Classic Cars Coloring Book

James Delaney

Greetings, and welcome to the world of classic cars!

My name is James, and I'm thrilled to share with you my brand-new classic car coloring book. Each page features a detailed illustration of the most iconic and beloved classic cars that I know you love, along with an interesting fact for each one.

From the sleek and elegant Aston Martin DB5 to the powerful and rugged Ford Mustang, this coloring book has it all.

I've put a lot of love and care into creating this coloring book, and I hope it will bring endless joy and relaxation to classic car enthusiasts everywhere. As you color in each page, you'll feel as though you're right there behind the wheel, driving through scenic landscapes and experiencing the thrill of these legendary cars.

If you enjoy this coloring book, I would be ever so grateful if you could leave a review on my Amazon page. Your feedback helps me tremendously. And if you like, please feel free to throw in a photo of your favorite coloring page. I'm dying to see your wonderful artwork!

I've also included 15 bonus coloring pages at the end, featuring classic 4x4s, sports cars and more, because I know just how much you love the aggressive Lamborghini Countach, or the iconic Land Rover Defender... so stay tuned for the next volume!

Thank you again for your purchase, and I hope you have a great time coloring and learning about these amazing classic cars!

Warmly,

James Delaney

PS Please bare in mind that while I've made every effort to ensure the accuracy of each illustration, some minor details may differ from the original cars due to artistic interpretation.

INDEX

INDEX

BONUS PAGES

The Ford GT40 was created to challenge Ferrari's dominance in endurance racing, specifically at the 24 Hours of Le Mans.

FORD GT40

The Wrangler dates back to WWII when it was developed for military, gaining a reputation for toughness and durability.

JEEP WRANGLER

The Audi R8 has become a symbol of elegance and superhero style thanks to its appearances in films like the "Iron Man" series.

AUDI R8

The DB5's powerful inline-six engine and exquisite form make it a hallmark of British automotive greatness.

ASTON M...

Use this color wheel to test out your colors and shades, with darker colors on the outside, and lighter colors in the center.

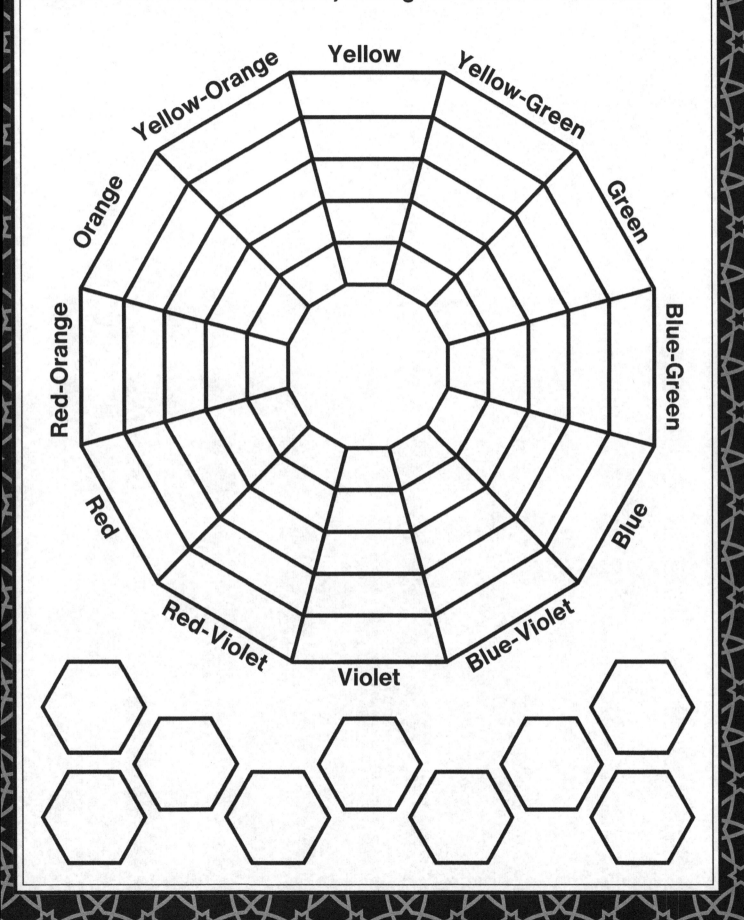

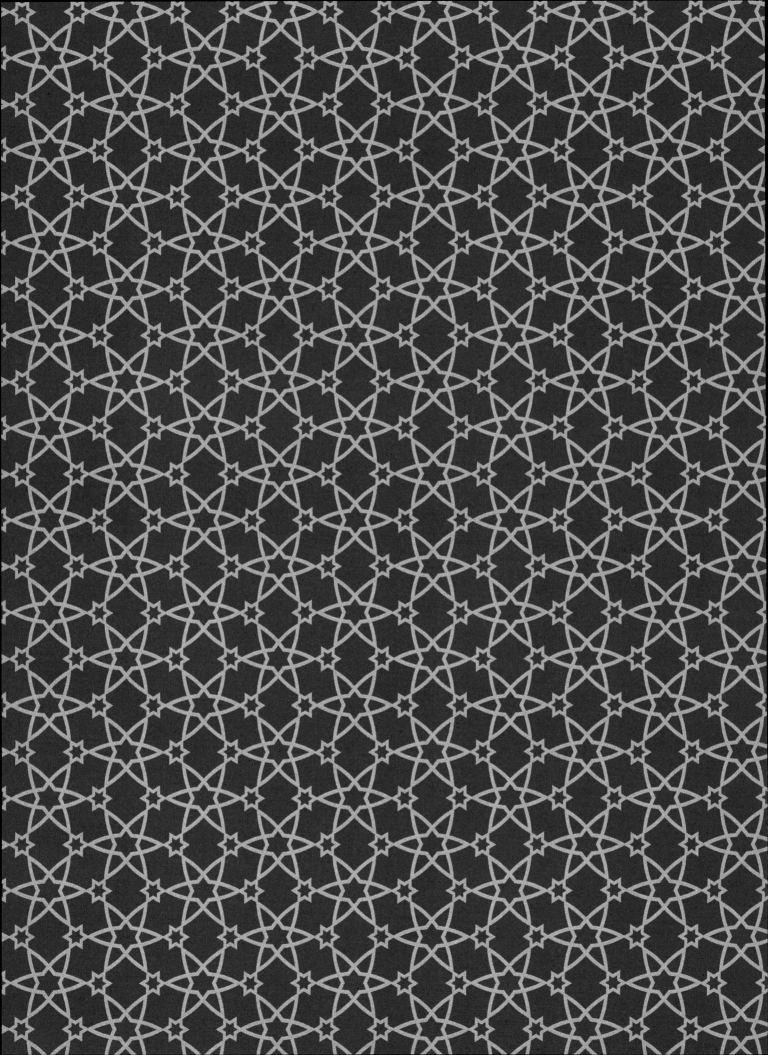

The '57 Corvette was the first American car with fuel injection.

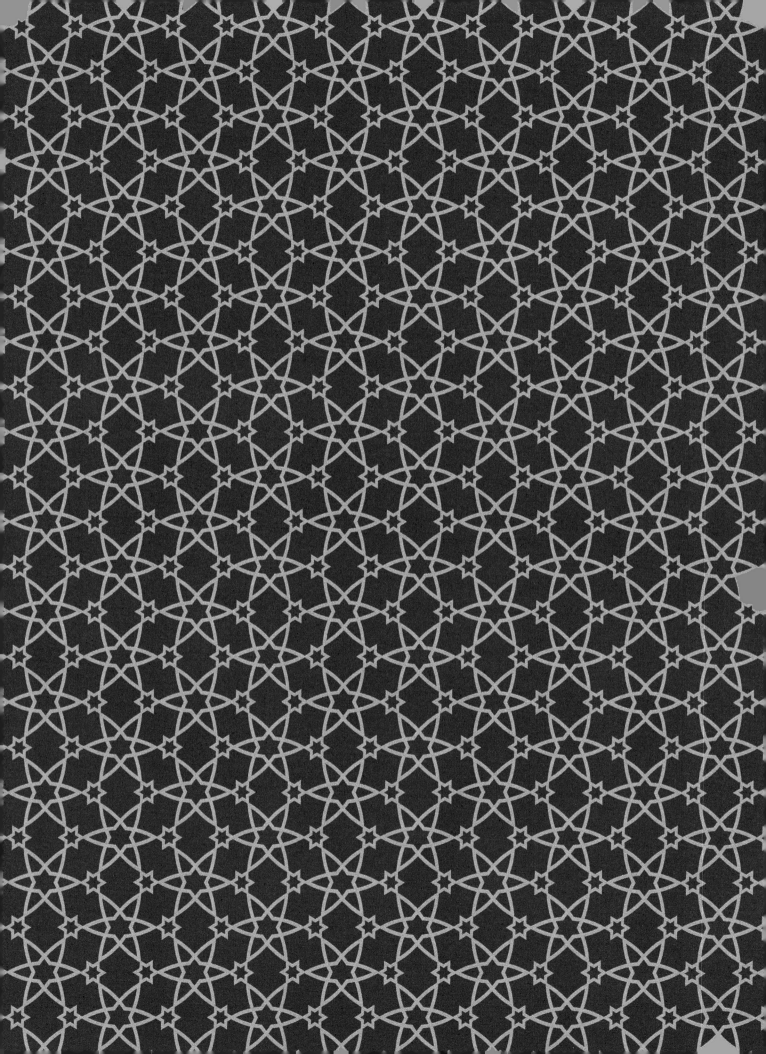

The '65 Mustang was an instant classic, selling over a million units in its first two years.

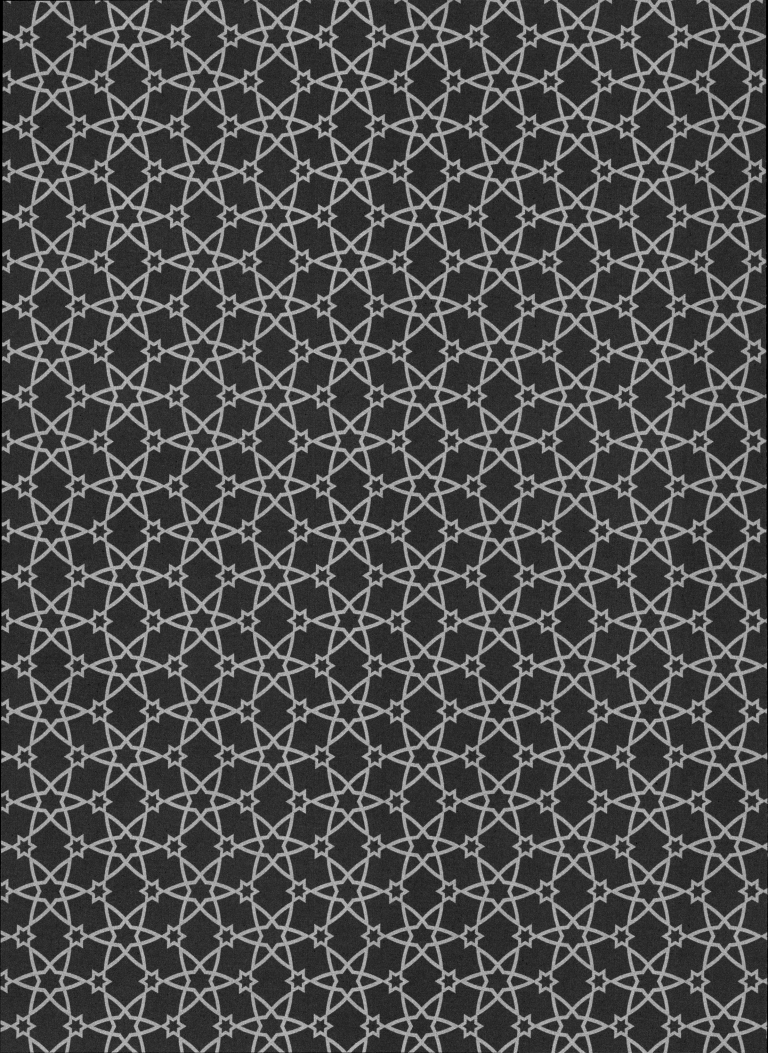

The DB5 is perhaps the most iconic Bond car, appearing in Goldfinger and other films.

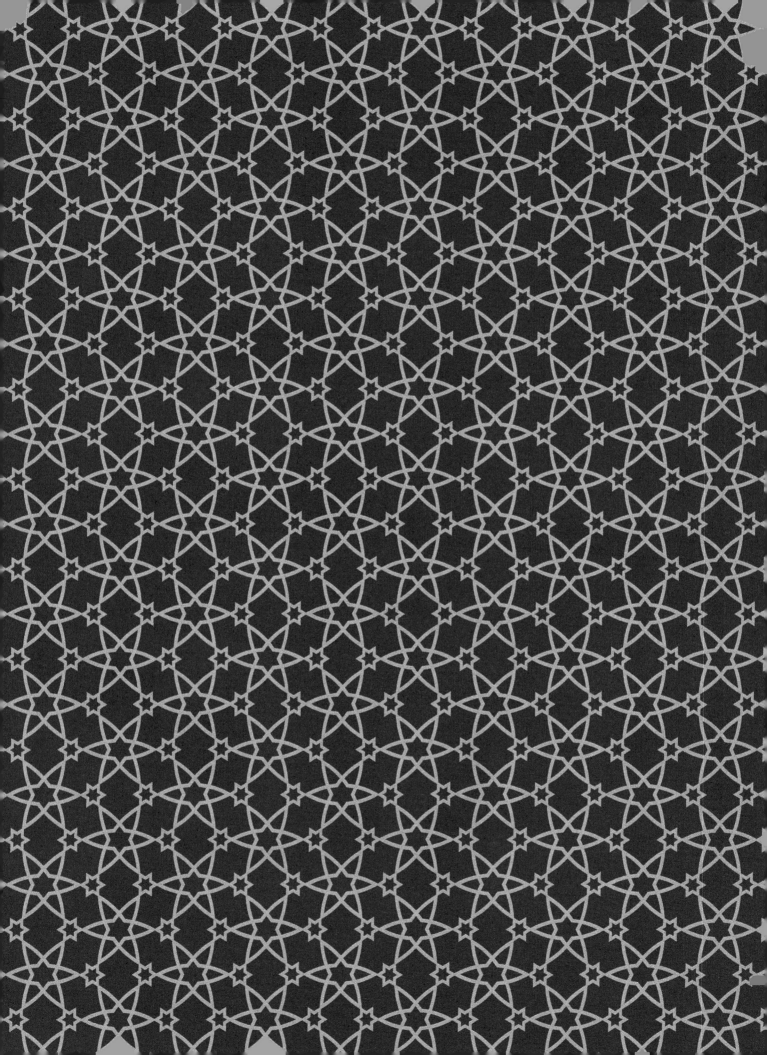

The '66 Skylark GS offered a 325-horsepower V8 engine and was the first Buick muscle car.

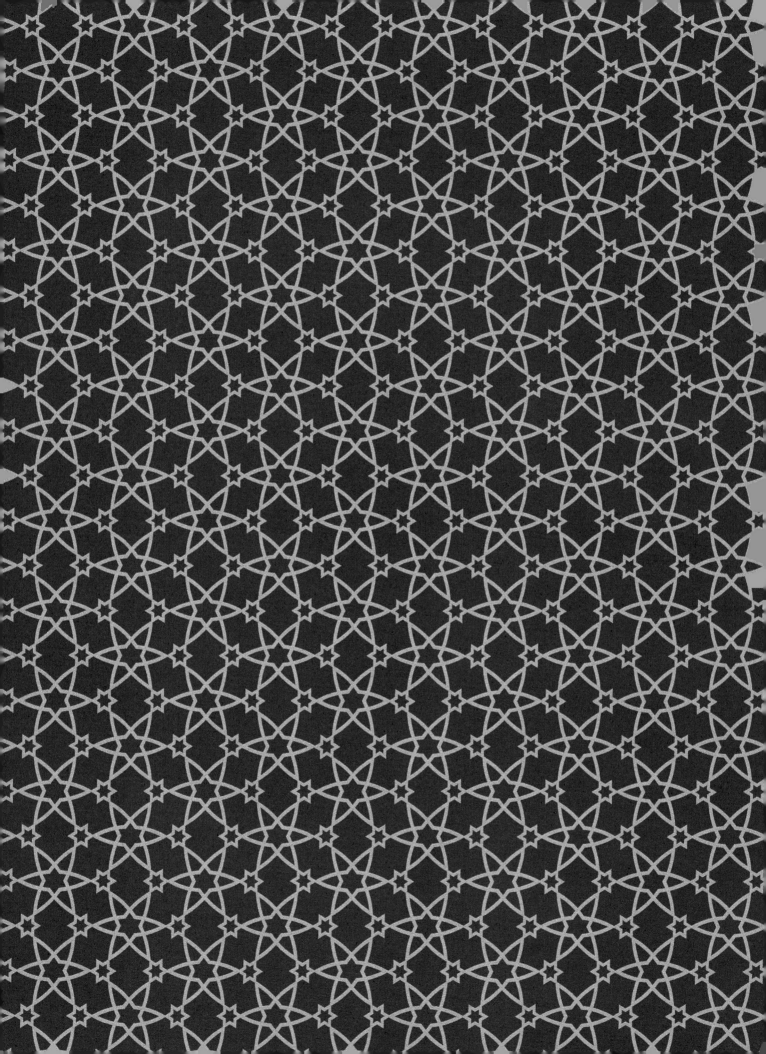

Bel Air was an innovative, luxurious car ahead of its time with power windows and air conditioning.

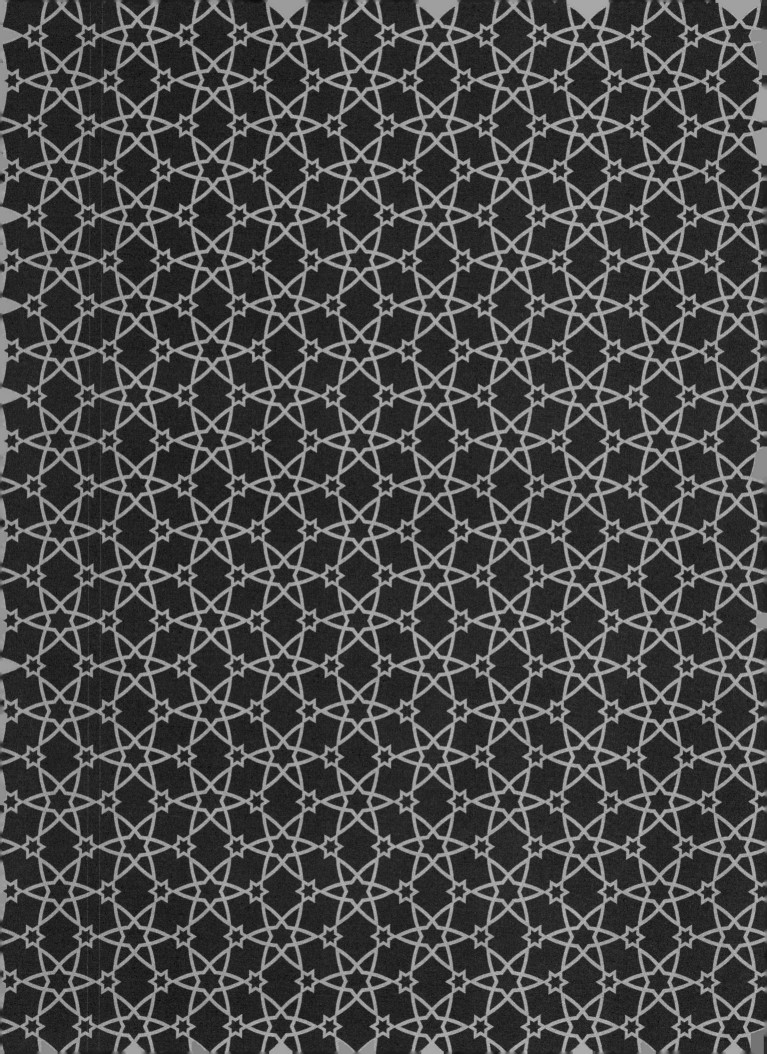

The Corvette Stingray was introduced in 1963 as a sleek and stylish sports car.

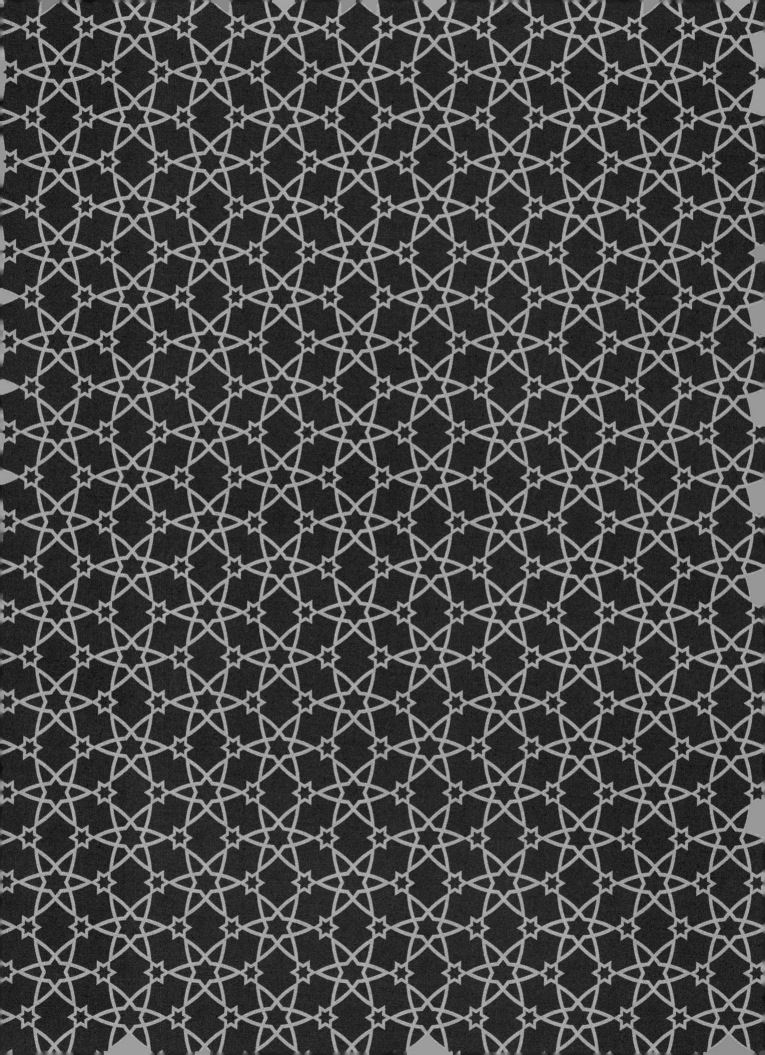

Chevy's iconic Impala debuted in 1958 with sleek styling and powerful V8 engine.

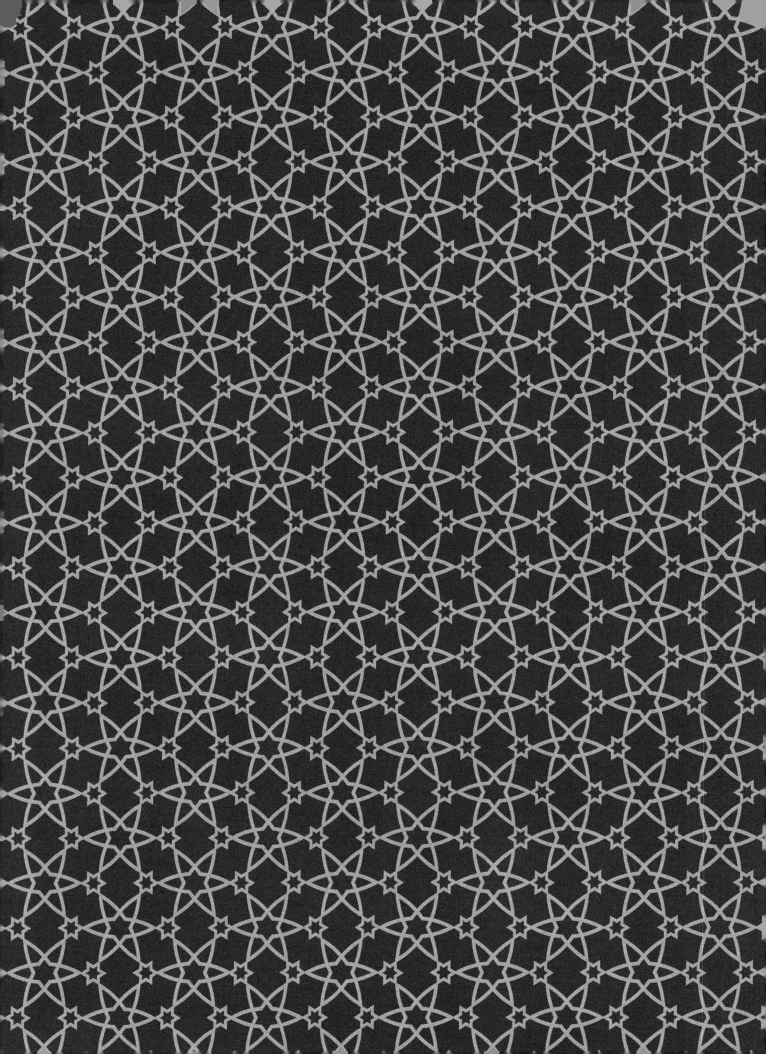

The New Yorker was a favorite among celebrities and politicians, including FDR and Elvis.

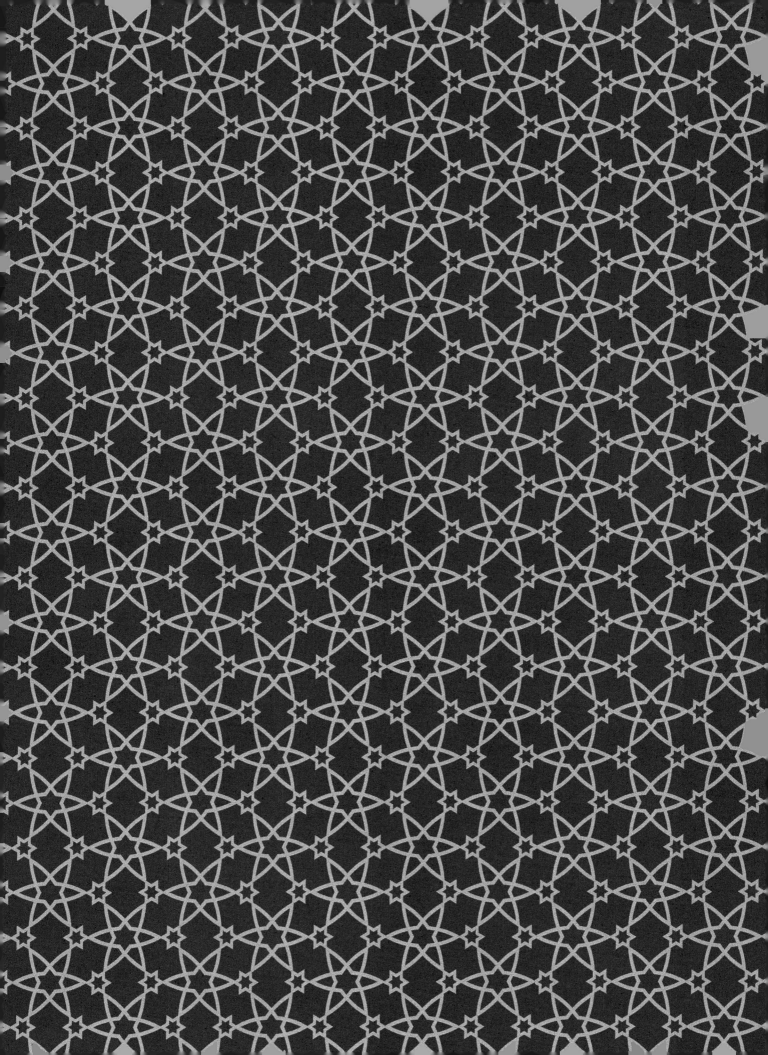

The DeLorean is a timeless icon due to its starring role in the "Back to the Future" films, and its iconic gull-wing doors.

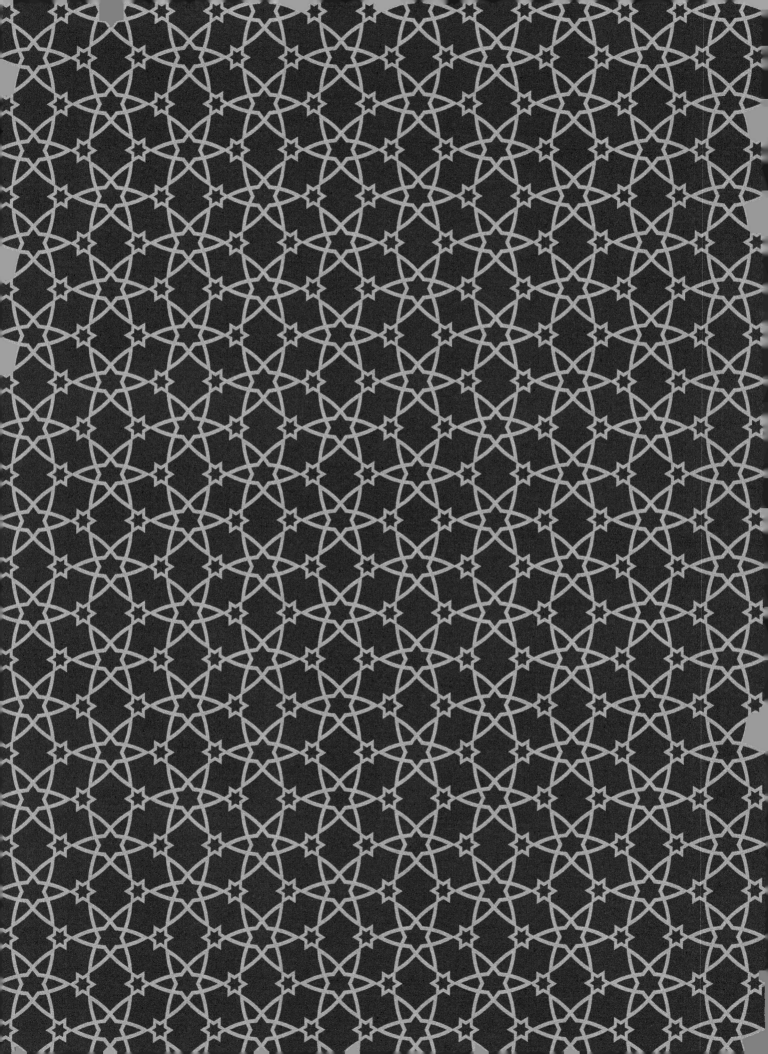

The Dodge Charger made its debut in 1966, evolving
into a legendary muscle car.

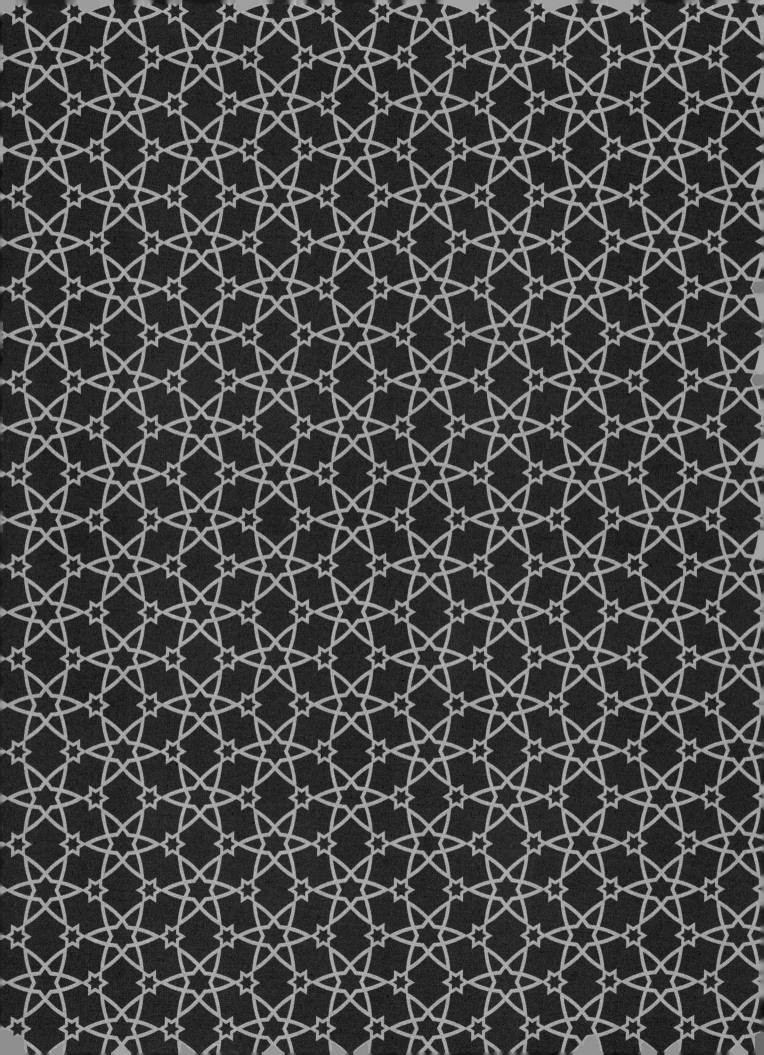

The Dart was popular in the racing world, with notable victories in NHRA and NASCAR competitions.

DODGE DART

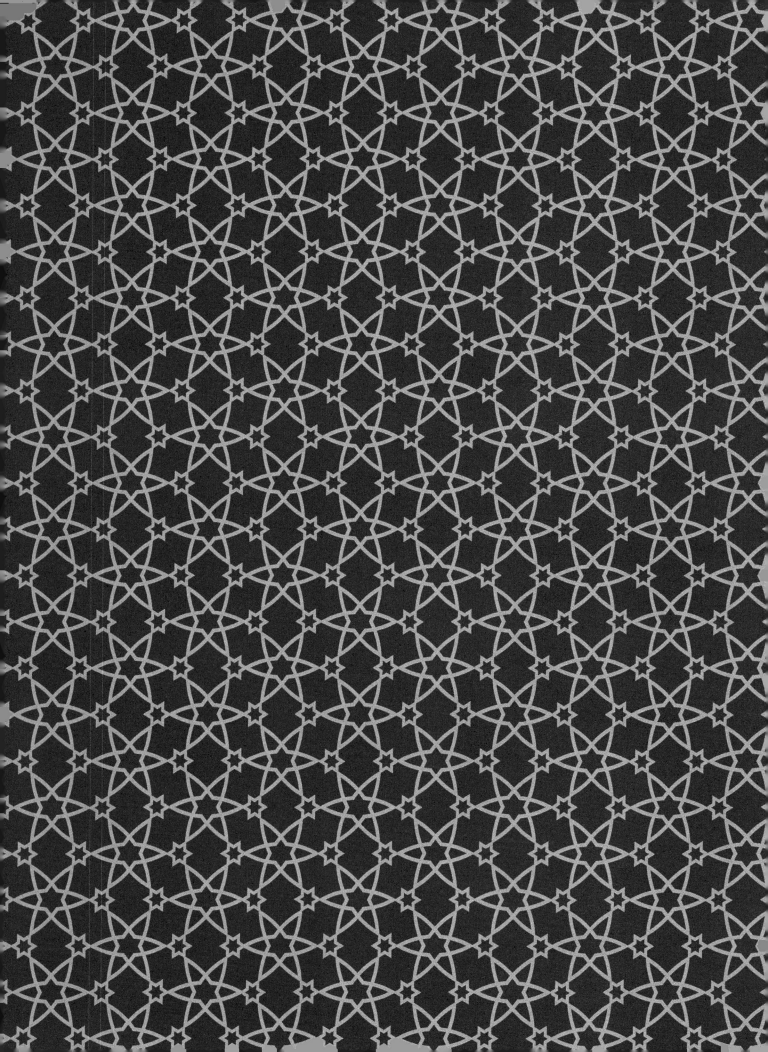

The Thunderbird was the inspiration behind the naming of the "T-Birds" in the musical Grease.

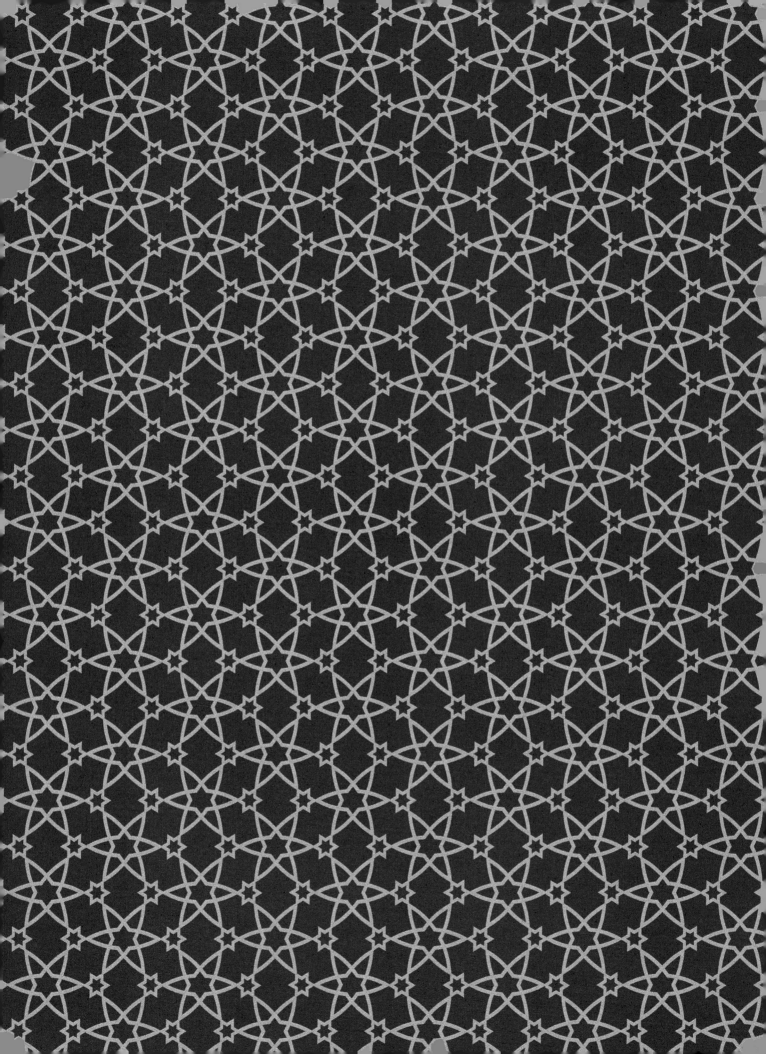

Ford's Thunderbird was an iconic luxury car made from 1955 to 2005.

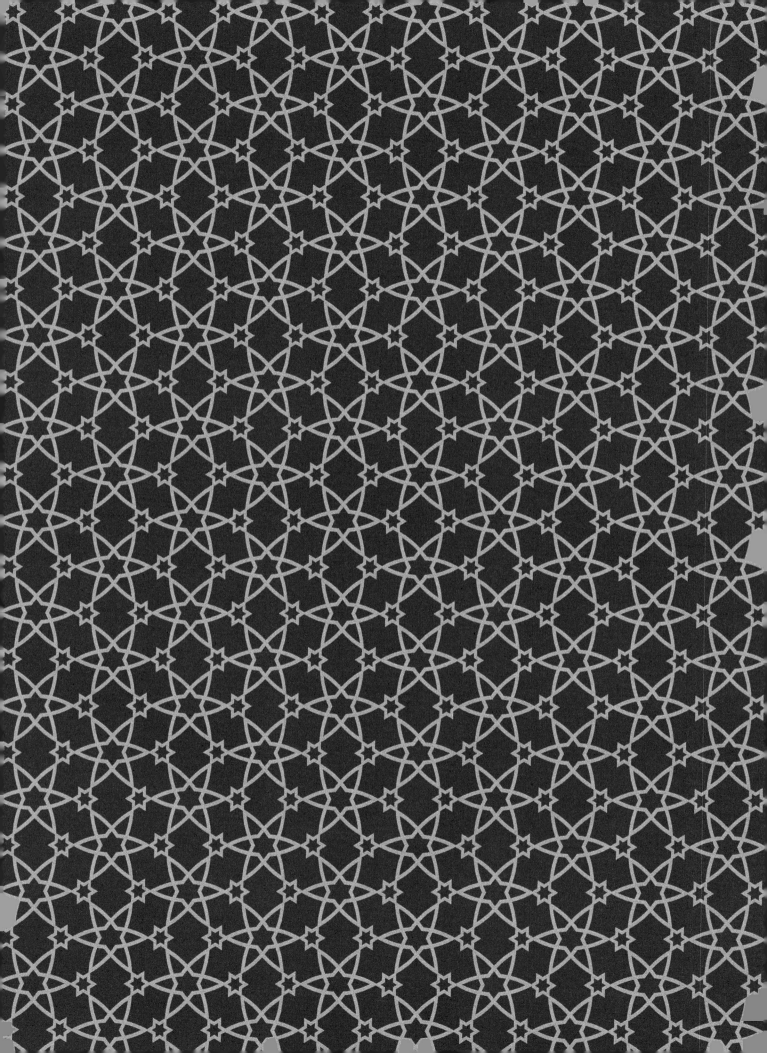

The Lotus Esprit famously featured in the James Bond film "The Spy Who Loved Me" as a submarine car.

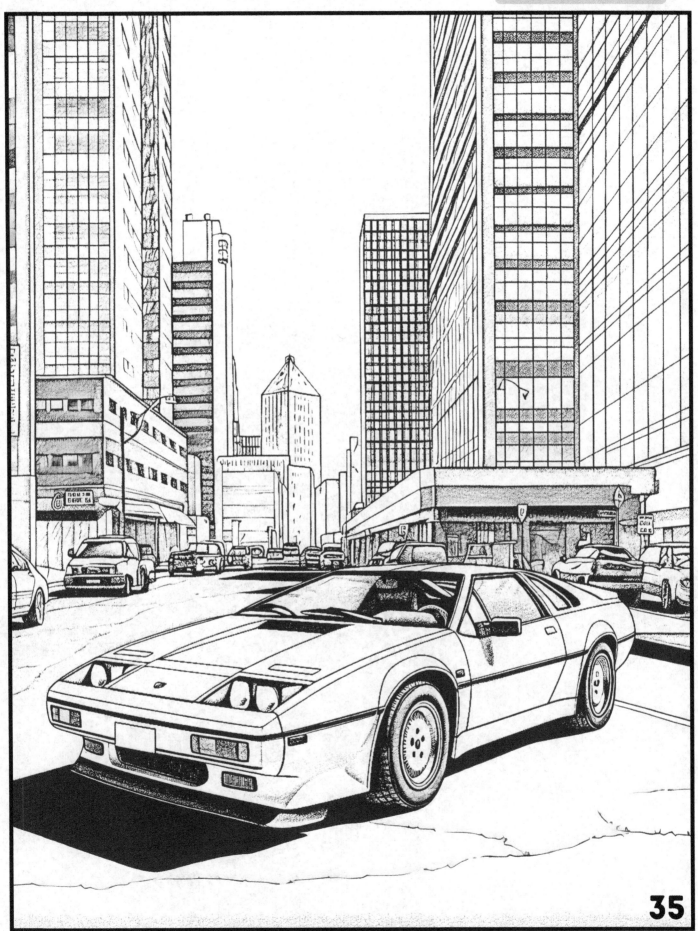

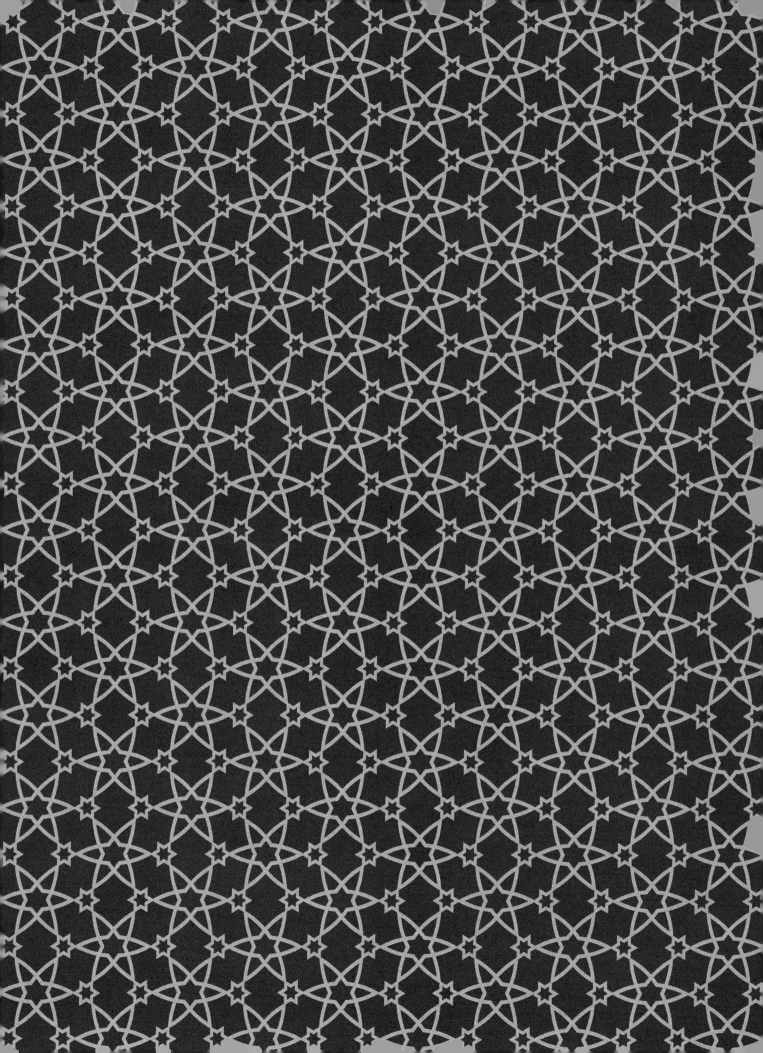

The Mercedes-Benz 300SL is widely regarded as one of the most beautiful sports cars ever made.

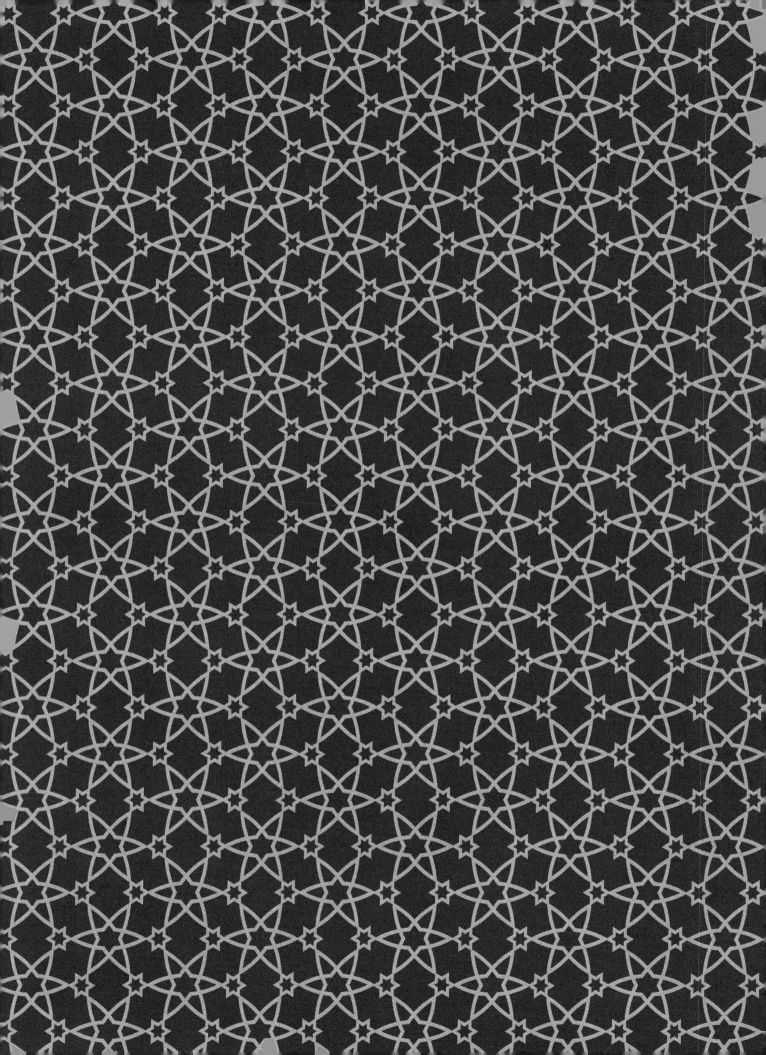

The Mini Cooper became famous for its small size and unique styling, and became a cultural icon of the swinging '60s.

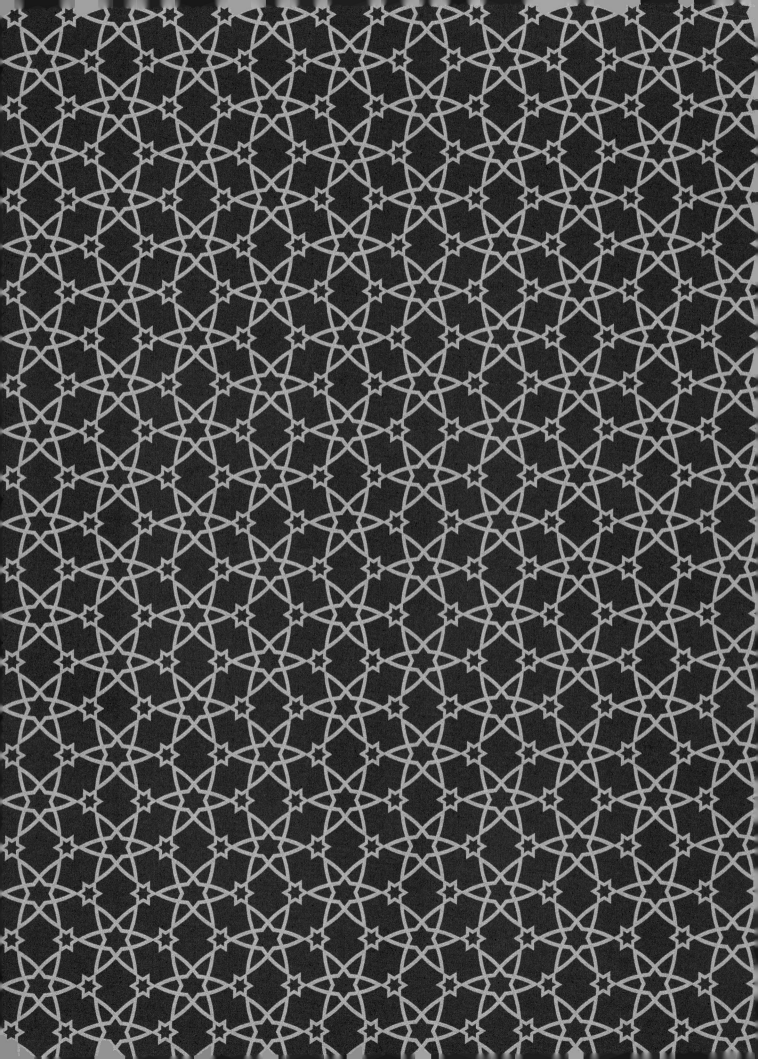

The Plymouth Barracuda was introduced in 1964 as Chrysler's response to the Ford Mustang.

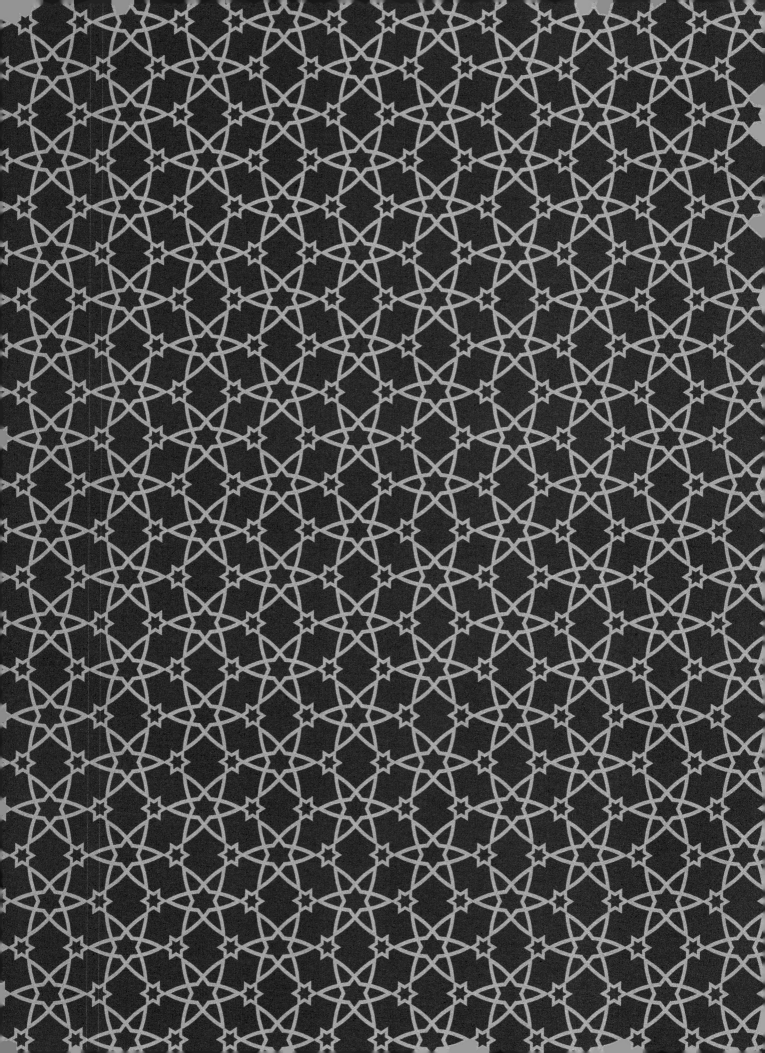

The distinctive horn was modeled after the "beep beep" of the Road Runner bird from cartoons.

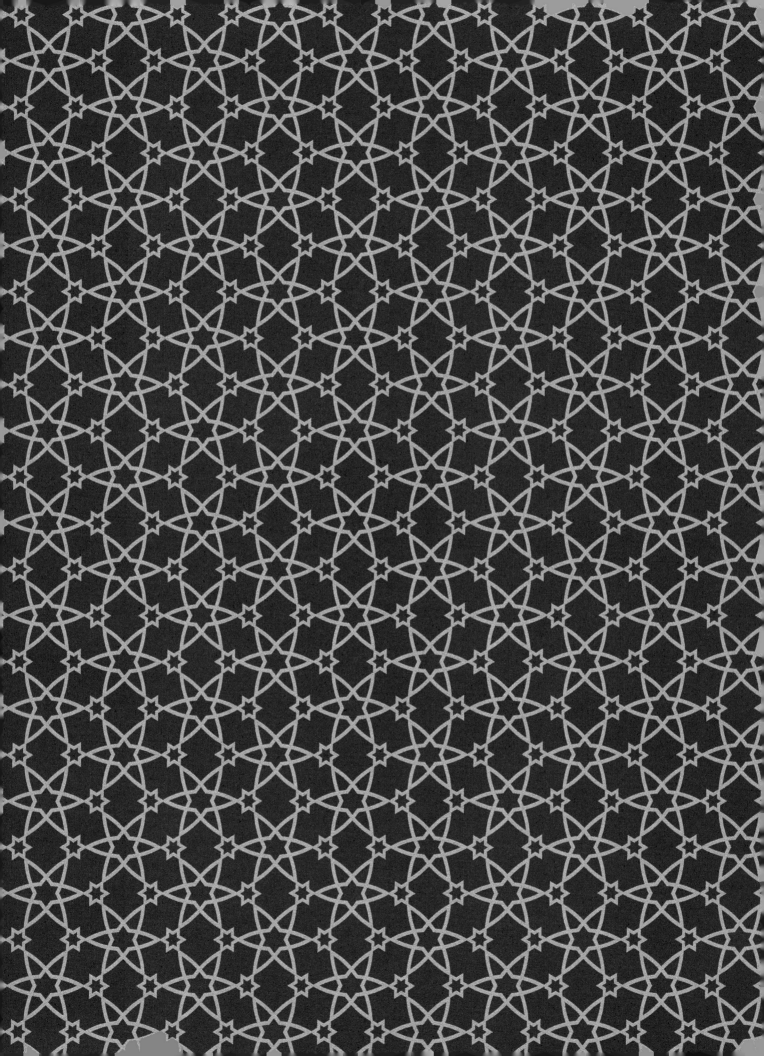

The iconic hood scoop was functional, providing cold air to the engine for increased horsepower.

PONTIAC FIREBIRD TRANSAM

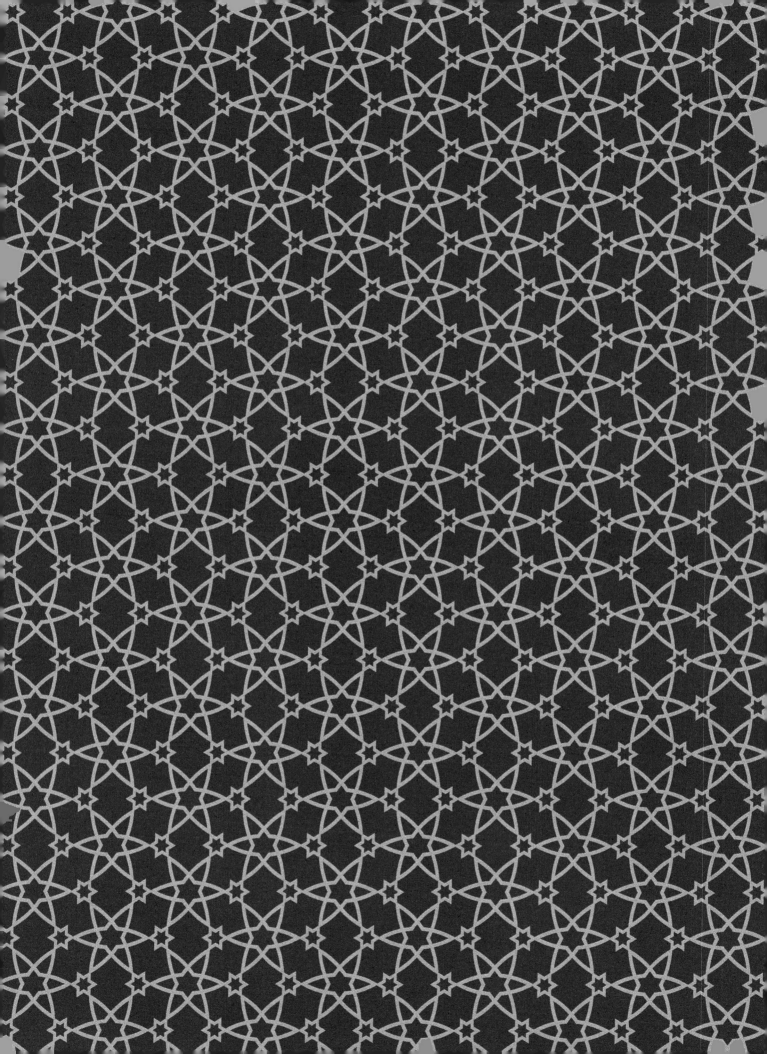

The Pontiac GTO is widely regarded as the first true muscle car, with a powerful V8 engine and sporty design.

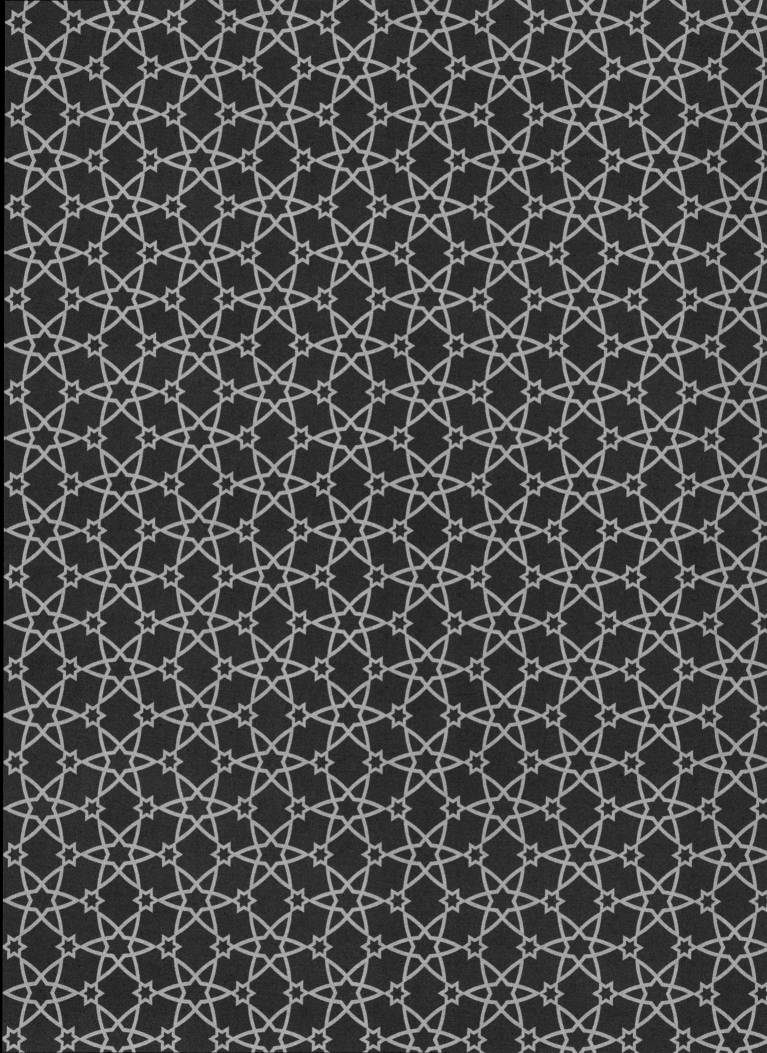

The 365's sleek, aerodynamic shape was inspired by the Volkswagen Beetle, which Porsche also designed.

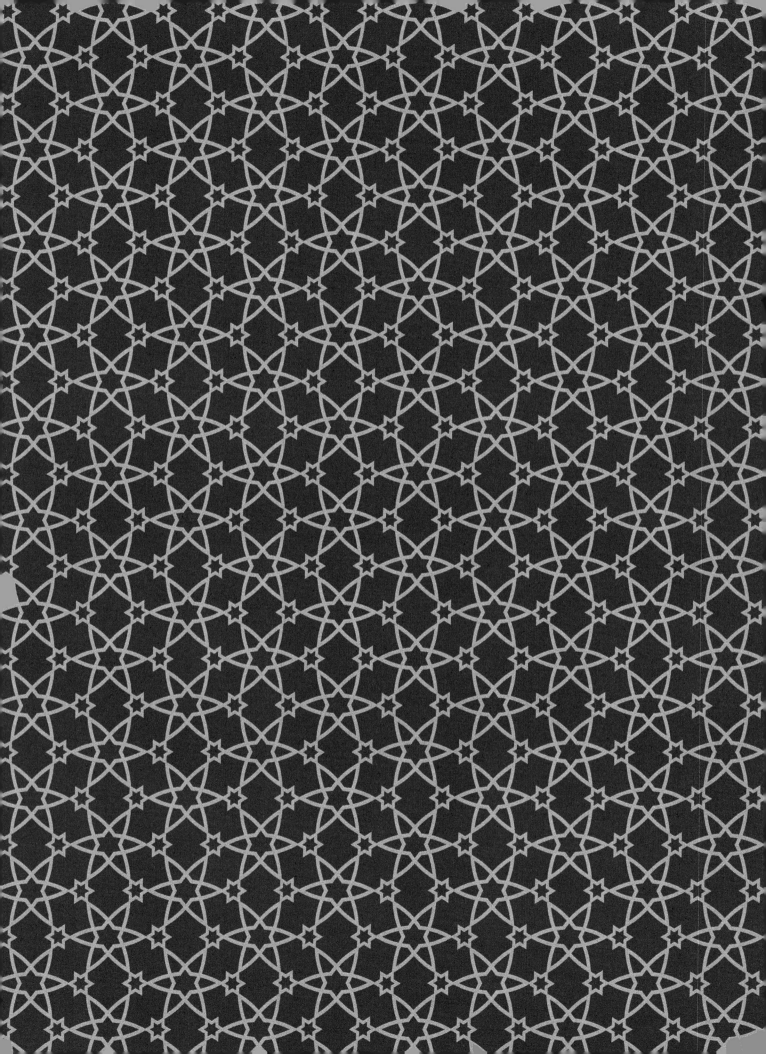

The 911 has been in production since 1963, making it one of the longest-running sports car models in history.

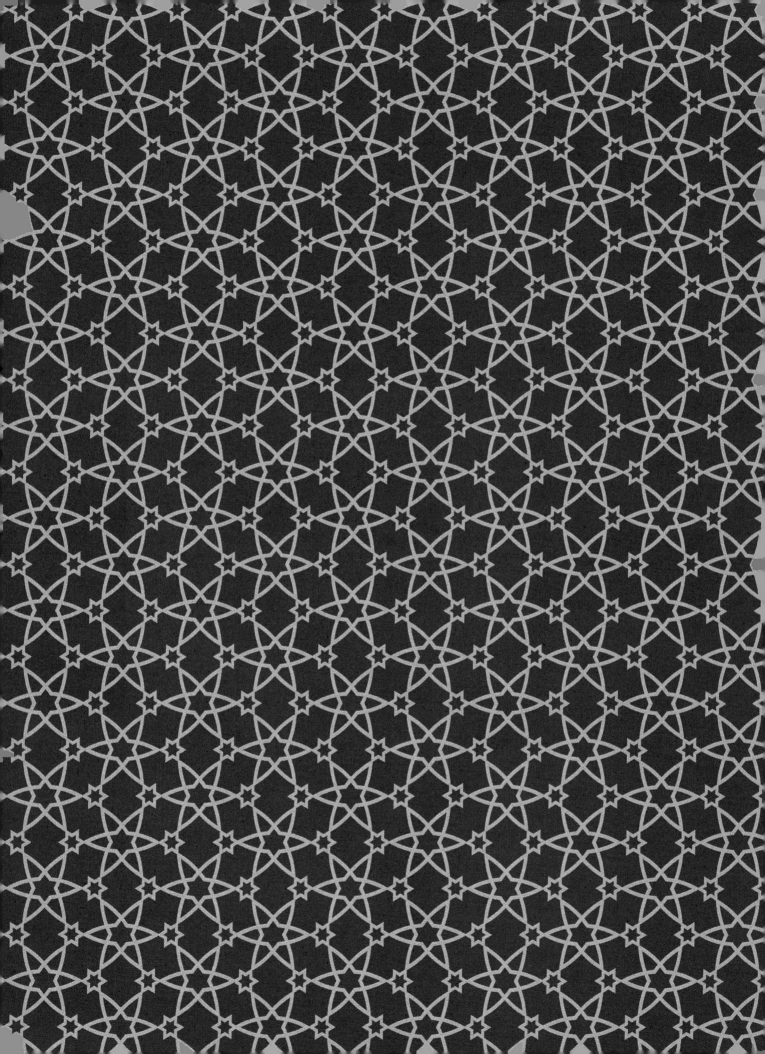

The Beetle was popularized in the 1960s, becoming an icon of the counterculture movement.

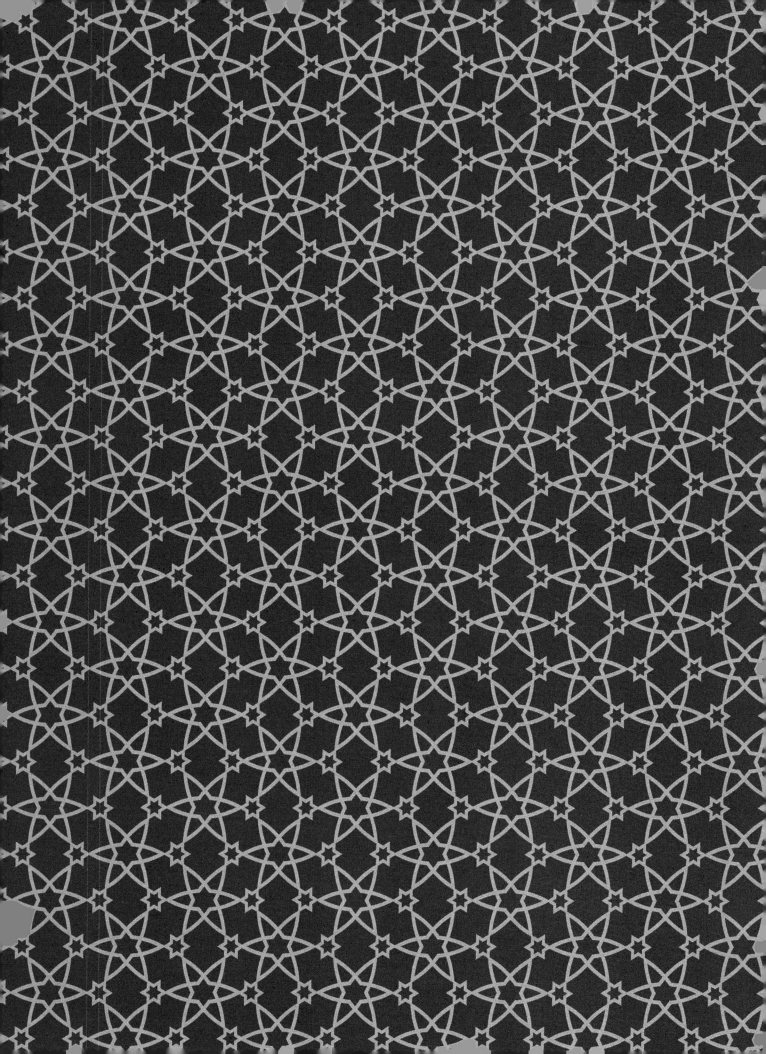

Only 1,000 Cobras were produced between 1962 and 1968, making it a rare and valuable collector's car.

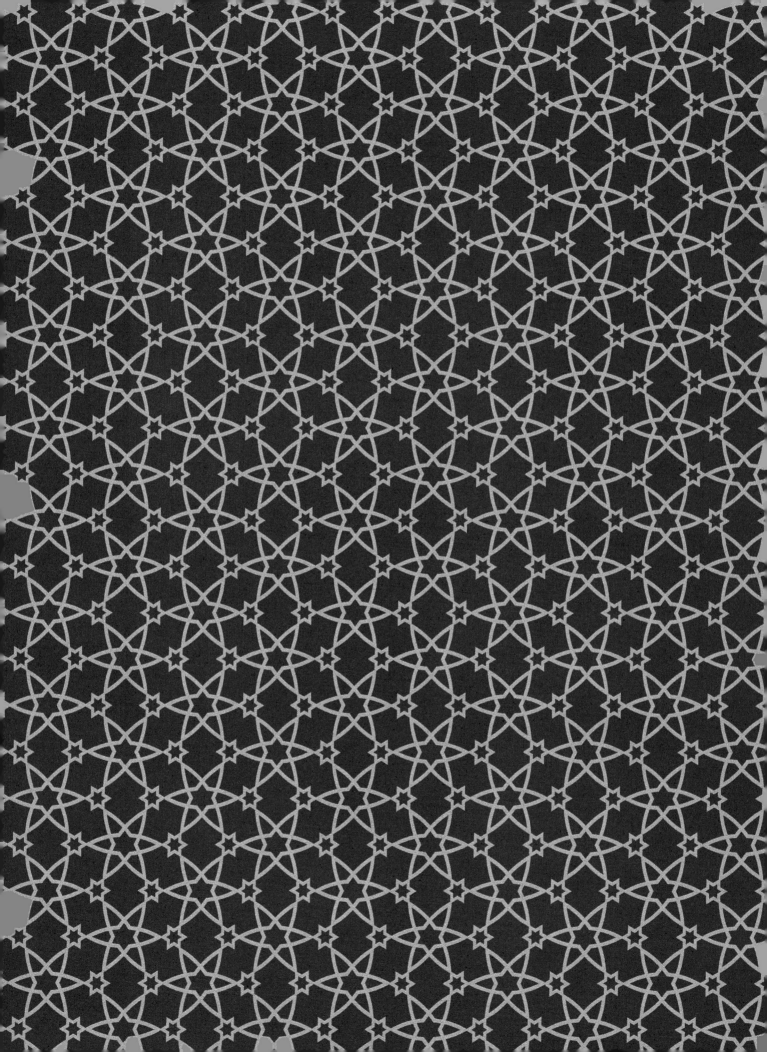

Mustang convertibles have been featured in James Bond movies and "Charlie's Angels."

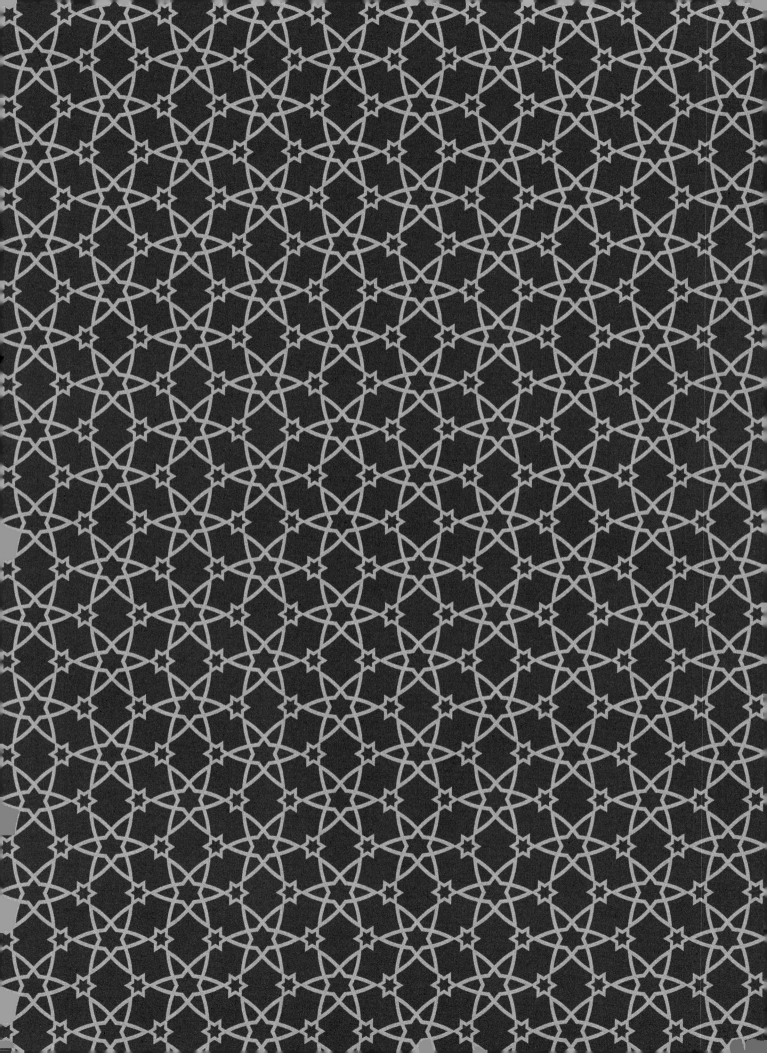

The 250 GTO's design, engine, and racing pedigree make it a favorite among collectors and enthusiasts.

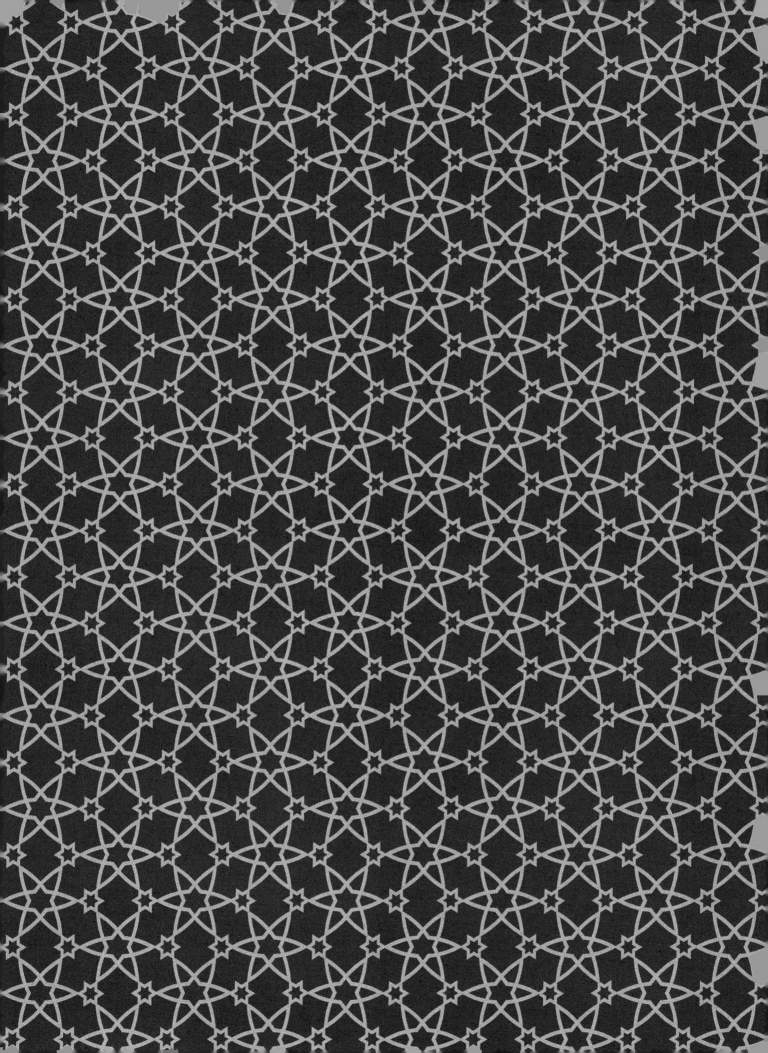

BONUS
PAGES

The versatile Defender's go-anywhere attitude makes it an adventurer's favorite.

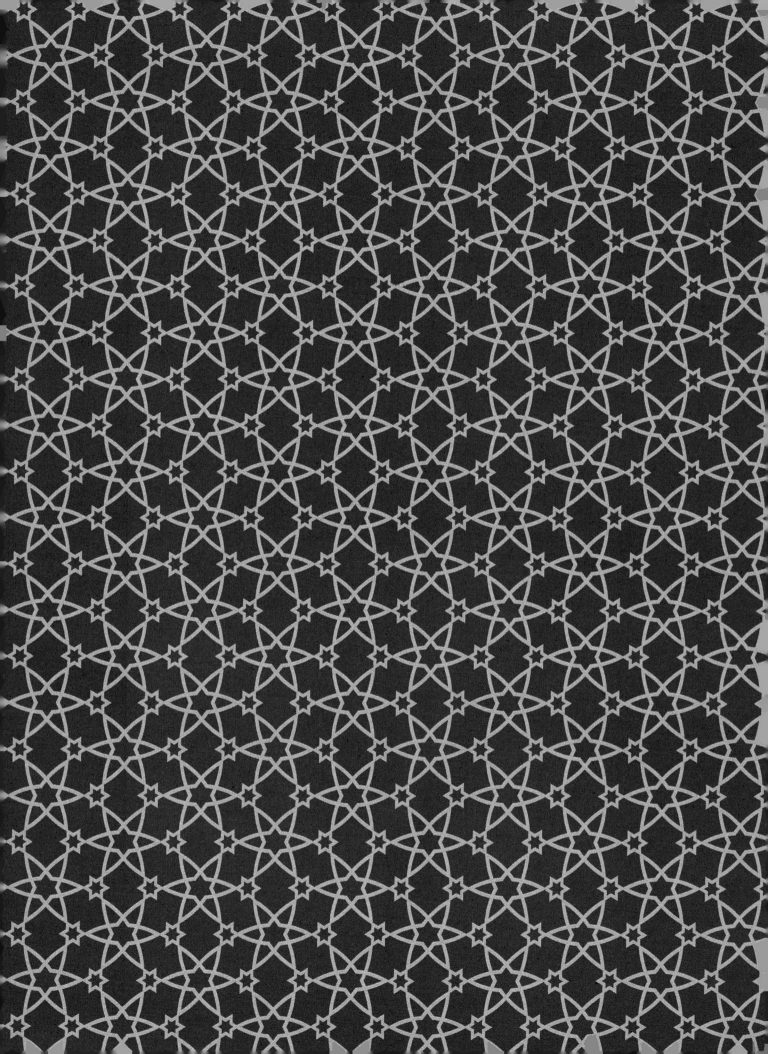

The 1941 Ford pickup is a classic American truck known for its sturdy build and iconic design.

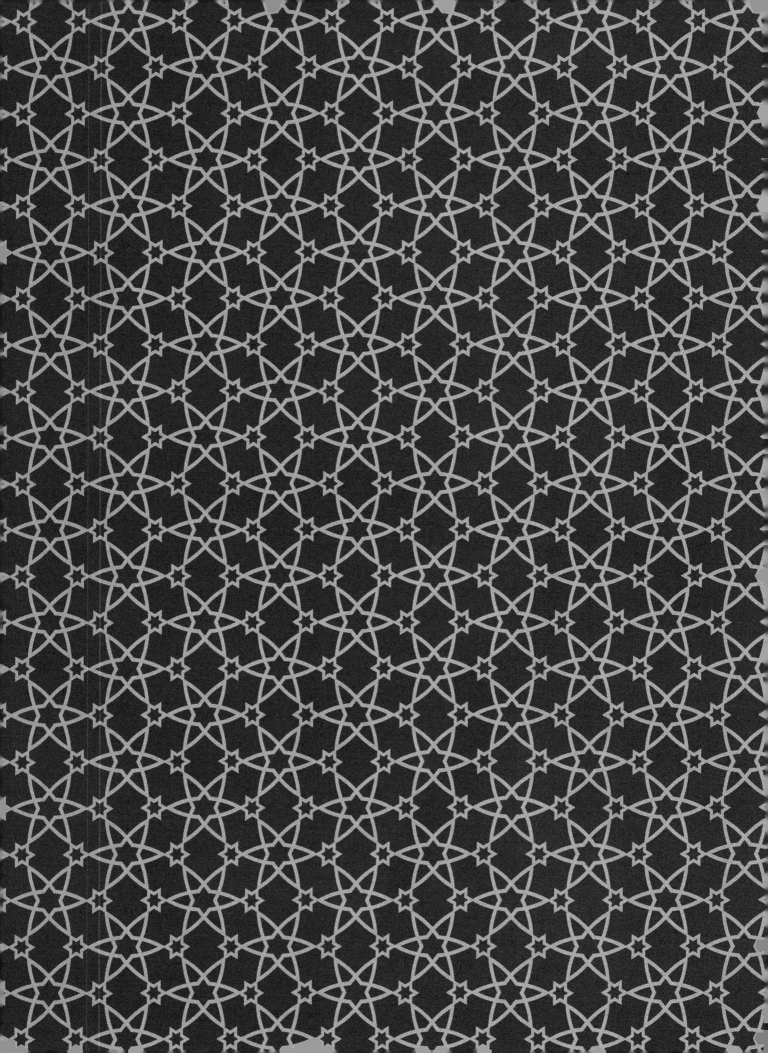

The Audi R8 has become a symbol of elegance and superhero style thanks to its appearances in films like the "Iron Man" series.

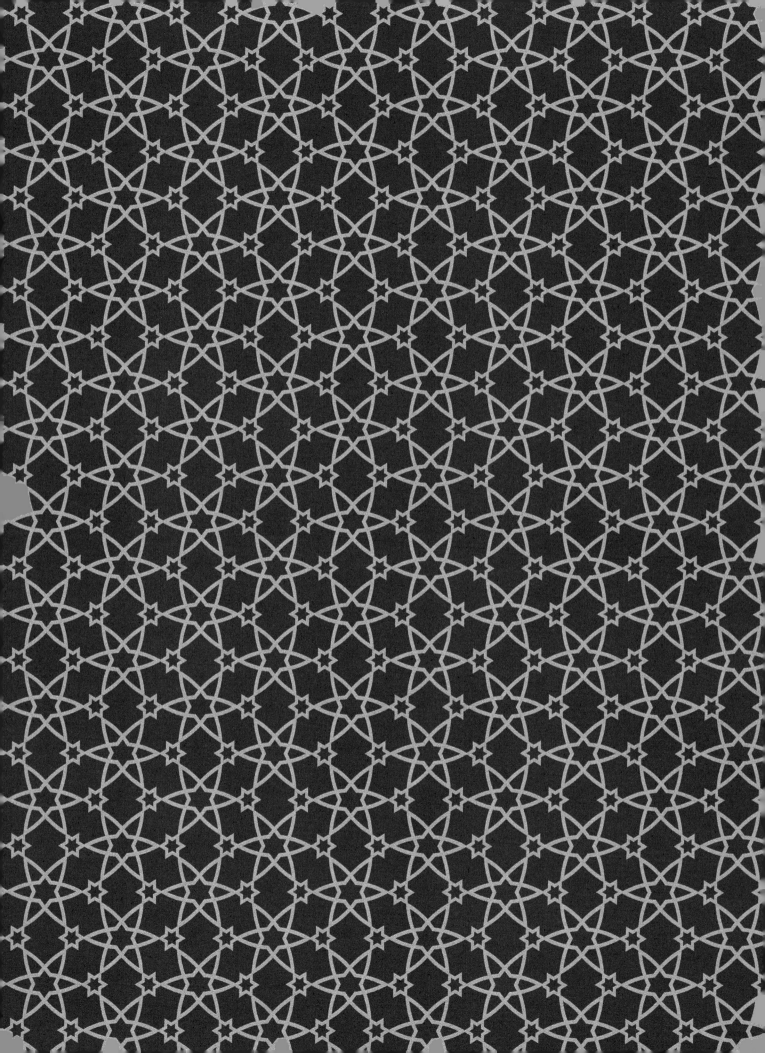

The DB5's powerful inline-six engine and exquisite form make it a hallmark of British automotive greatness.

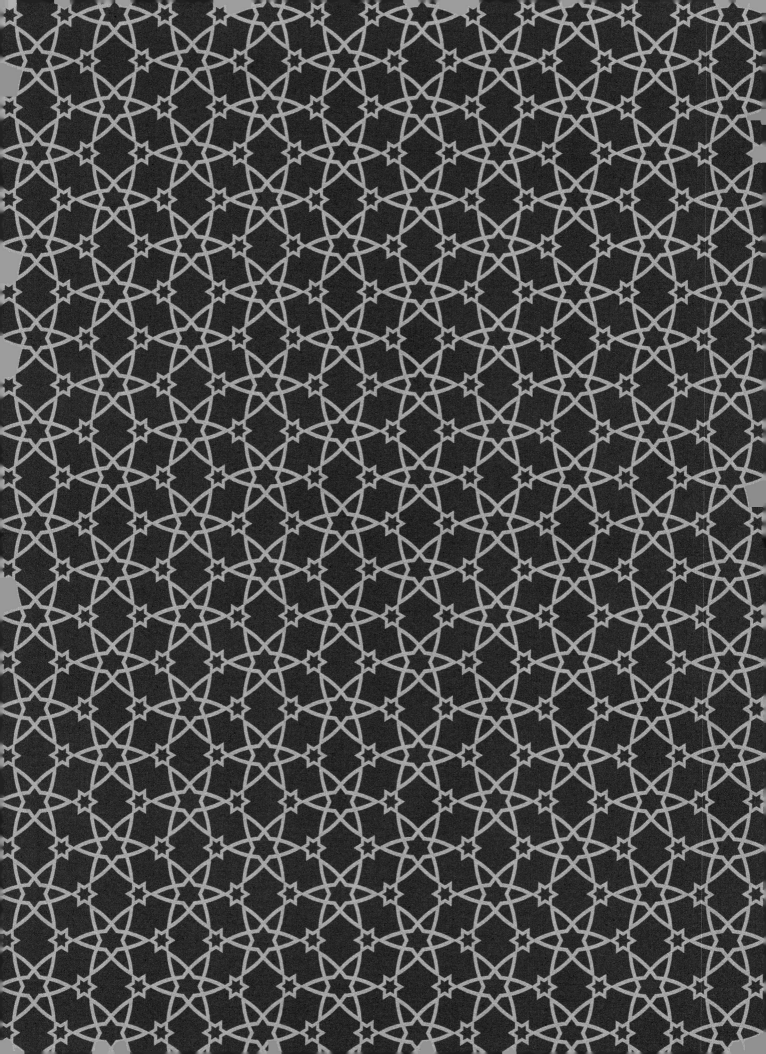

With its V12 engine and striking design, the Diabolo GT embodies the essence of Lamborghini's legendary supercars.

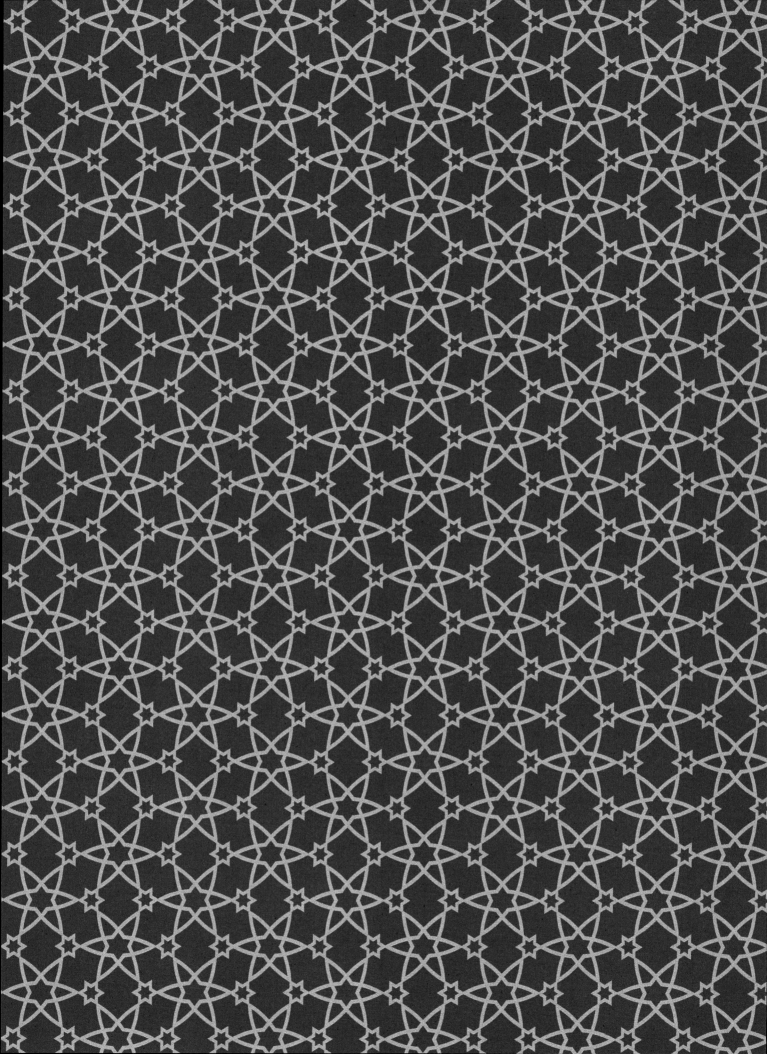

The Countach's bold and angular aesthetics
embodied the spirit of 1980s extravagance.

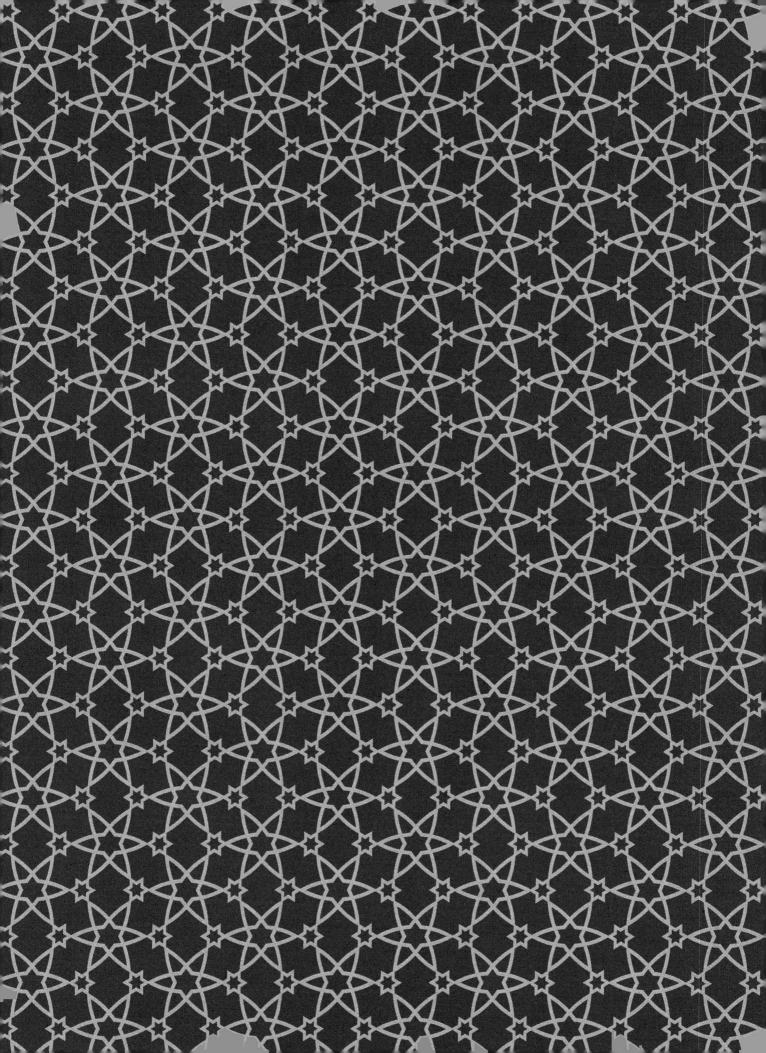

The SL500, with its retractable hardtop, is a symbol of luxury, performance, and style.

75

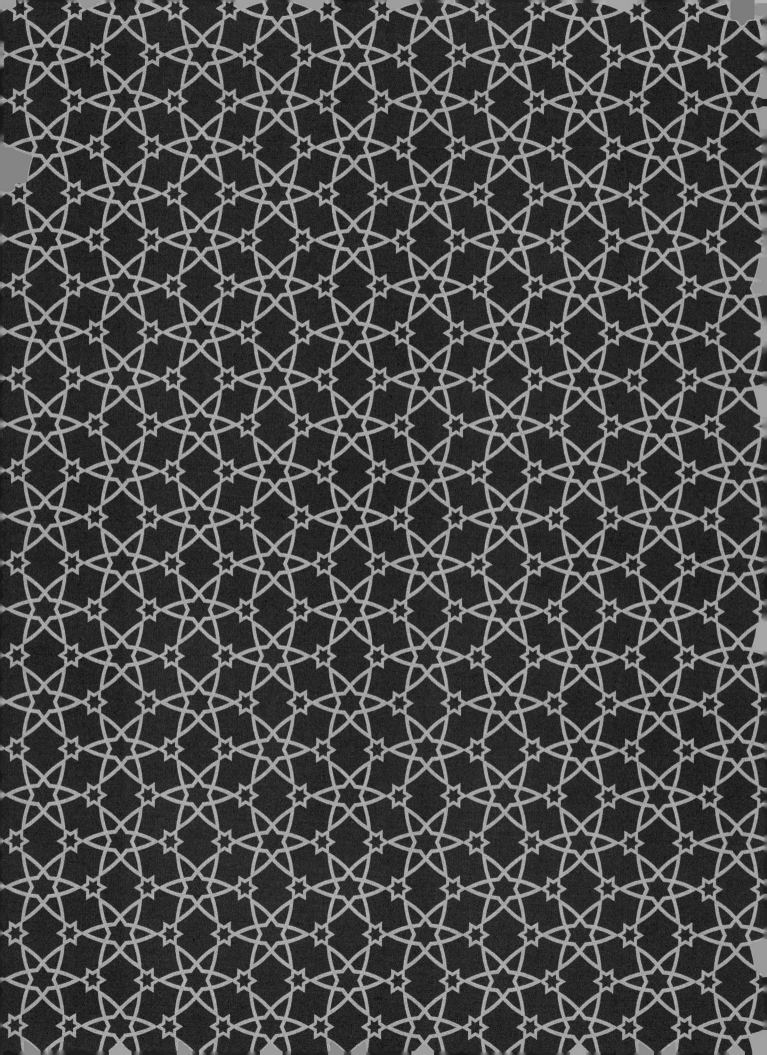

The Z4 Roadster combines cutting-edge technology, luxury features, and timeless BMW styling.

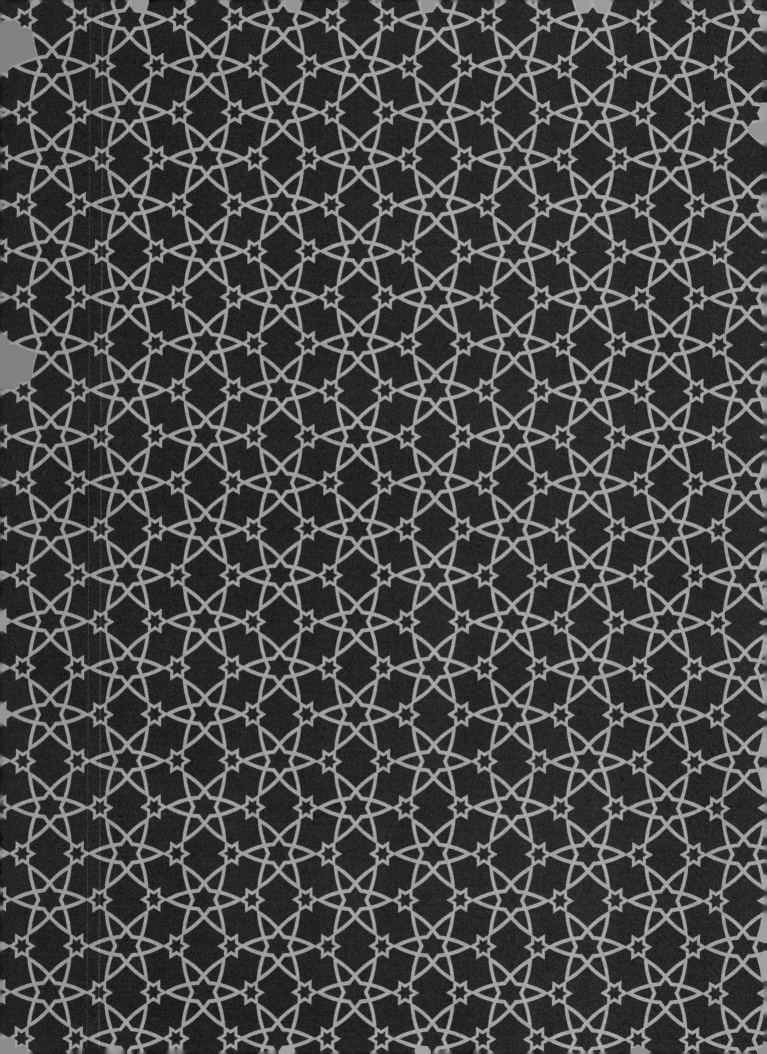

With its muscular body and high-performance V10 engine, the Viper delivers thrilling acceleration and exhilarating speed.

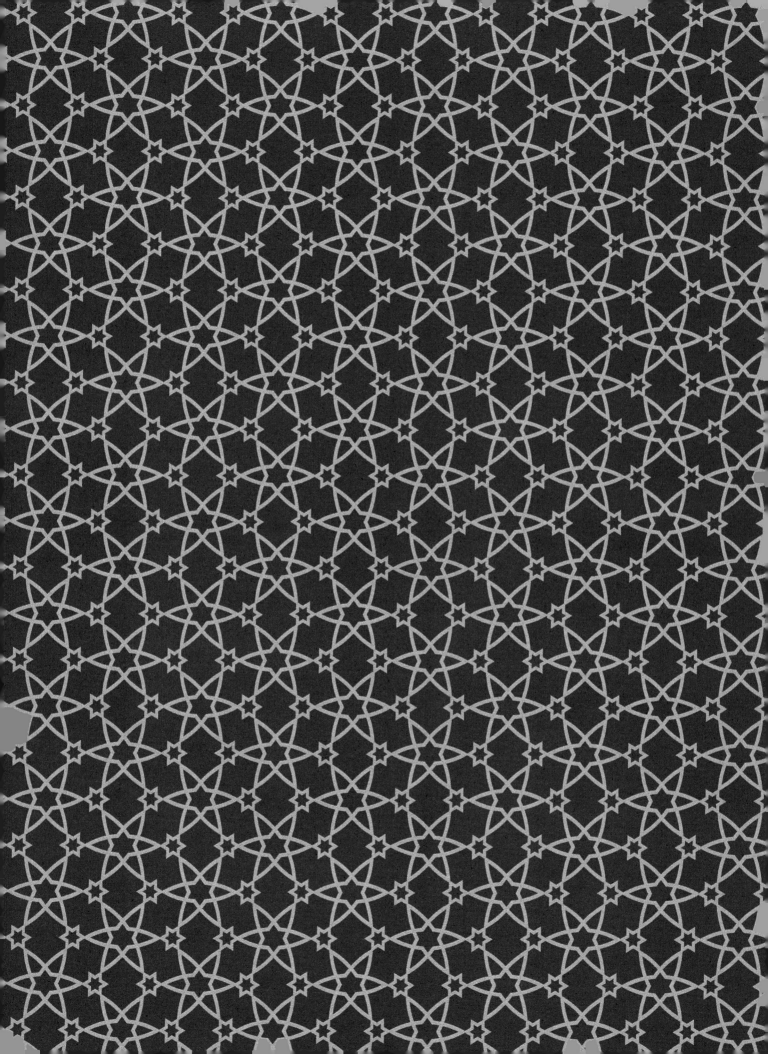

The Wrangler dates back to WWII when it was developed
for military, gaining a reputation for toughness and durability.

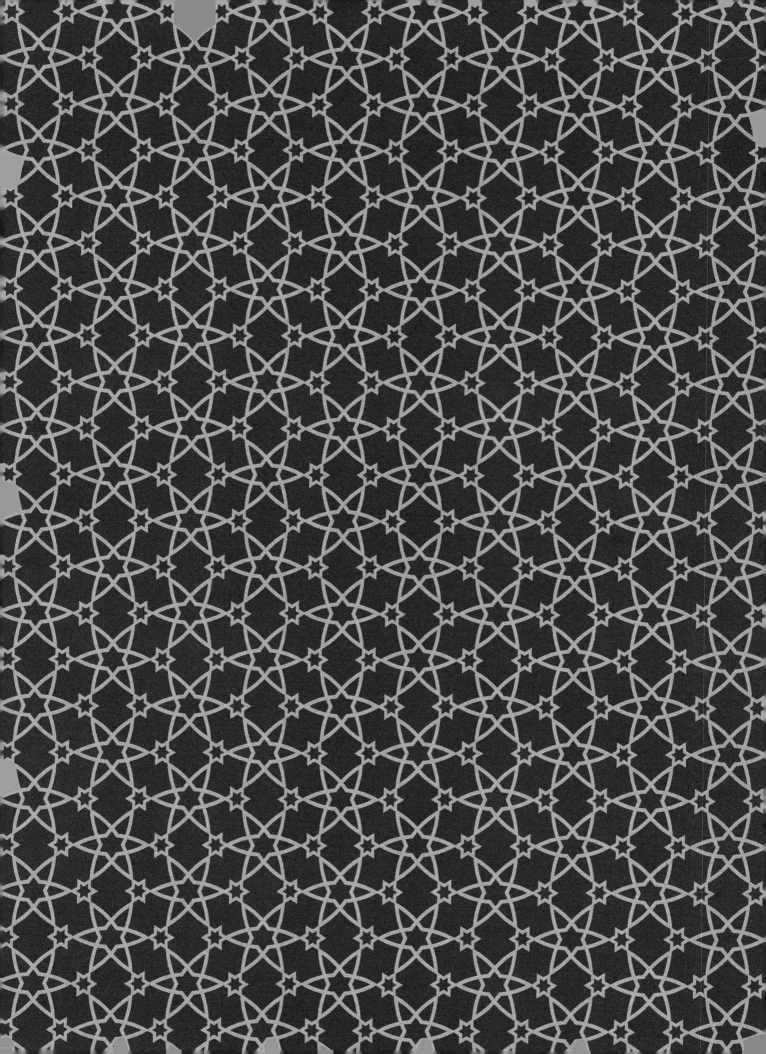

The Testarossa had a 4.9L flat-12 engine, reaching
a top speed of around 180 mph (290 km/h).

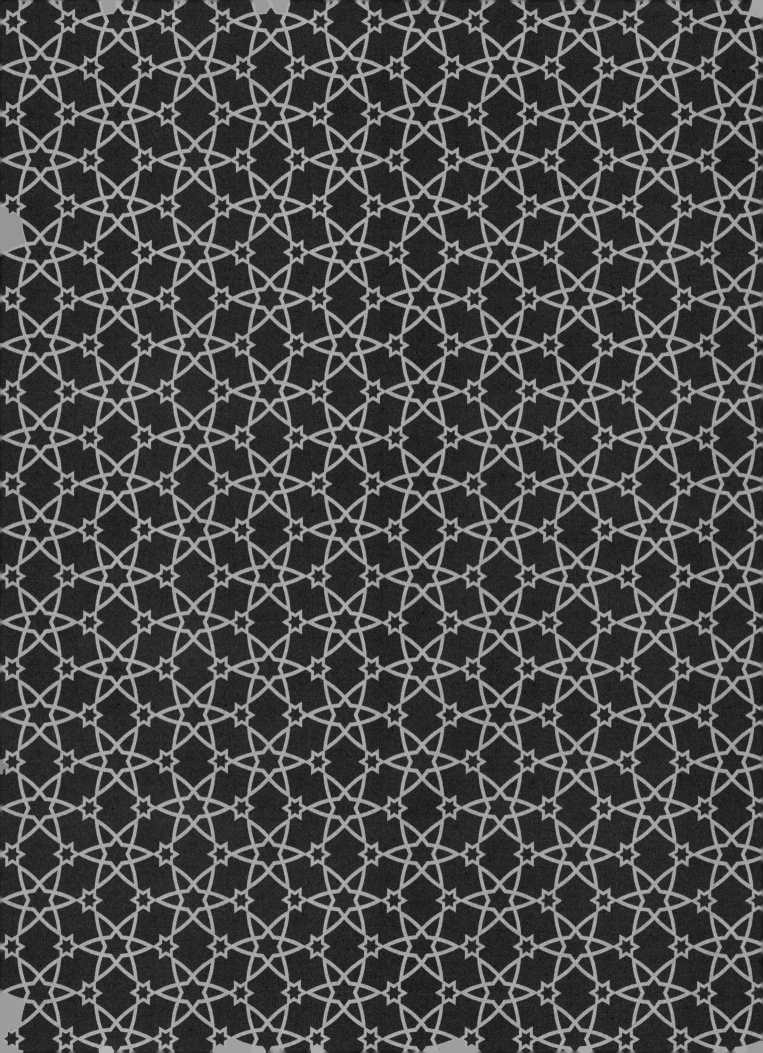

The Ford GT40 was created to challenge Ferrari's dominance in endurance racing, specifically at the 24 Hours of Le Mans.

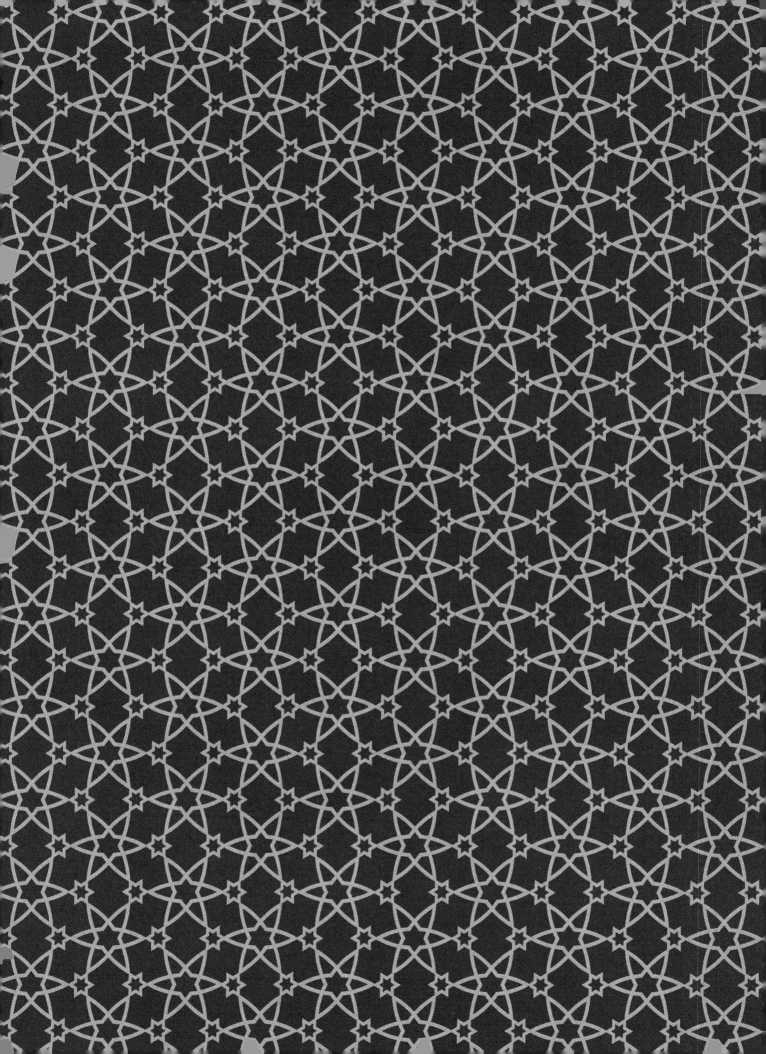

The NSX was the first production car with all-aluminum monocoque body for a lightweight and rigid build.

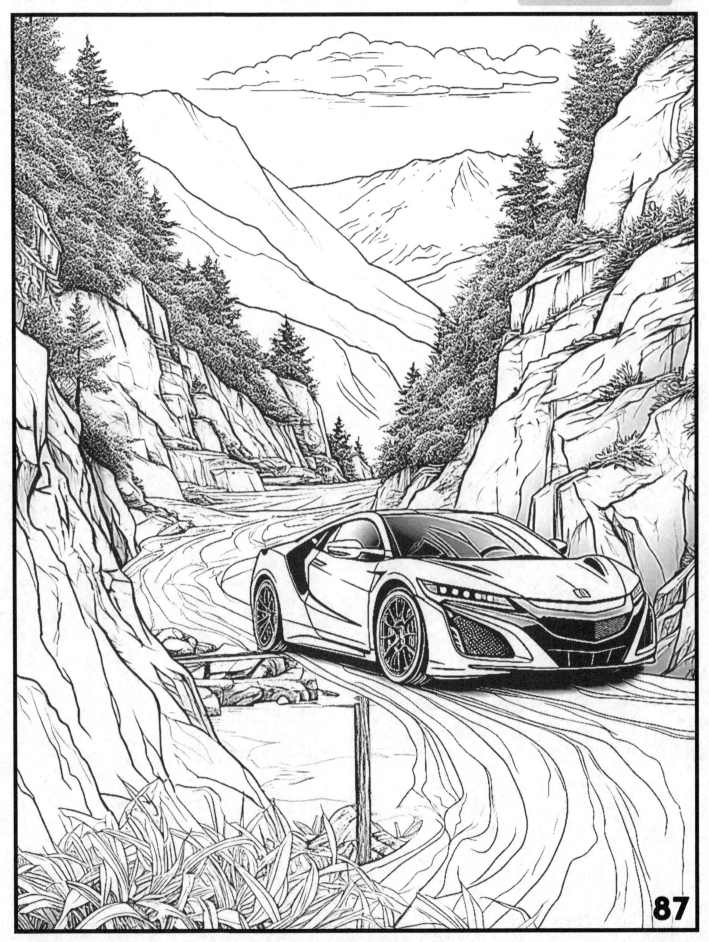

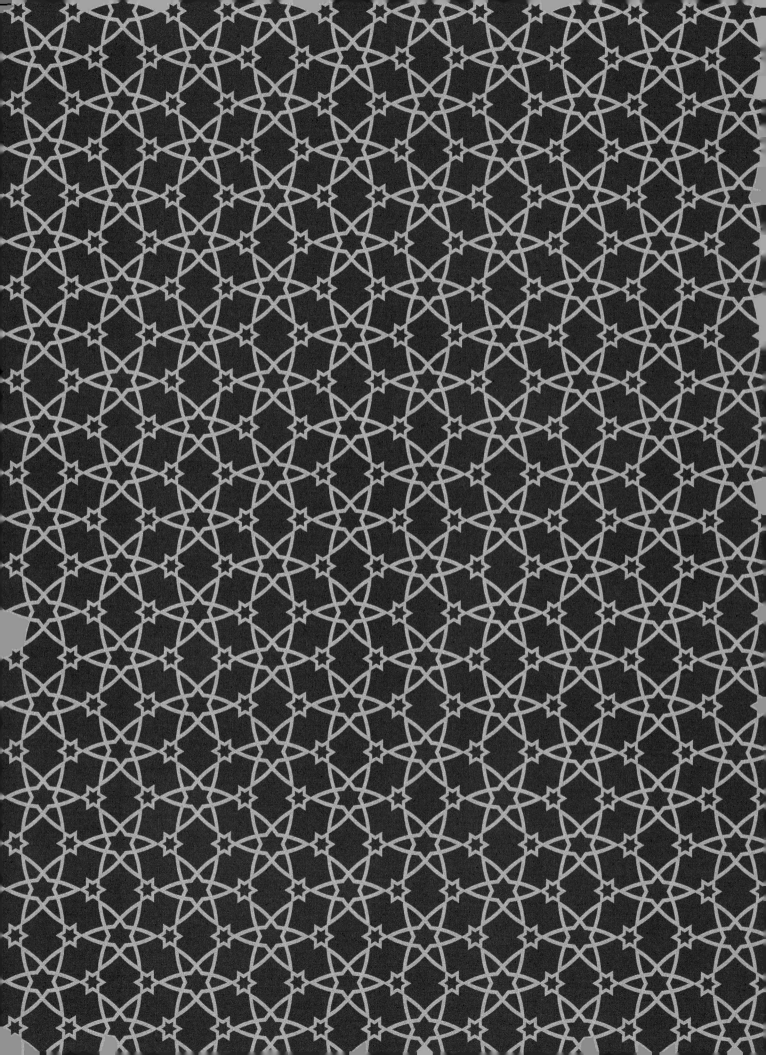

The Beetle's iconic design and charm made it a
global automotive and cultural symbol.

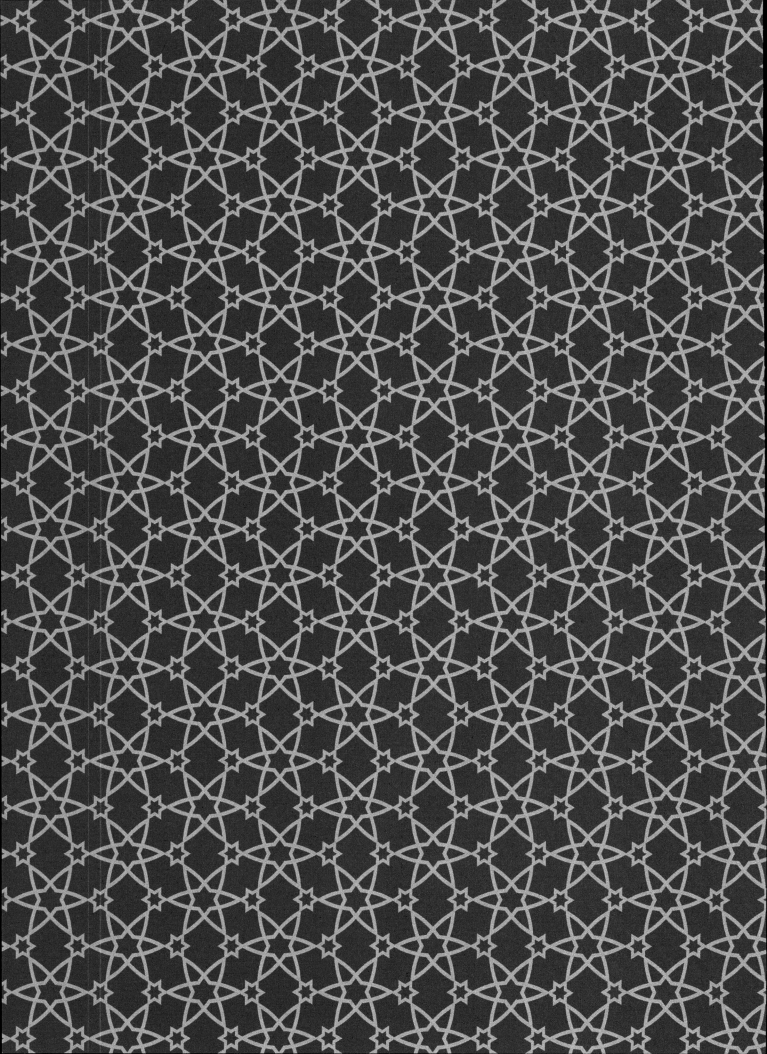